IT DOESN'T HAVE
TO BE LIKE THIS

IT DOESN'T HAVE TO BE LIKE THIS

Green politics explained

DAVID ICKE

GREEN PRINT

First published in 1990 by
Green Print
an imprint of The Merlin Press
10 Malden Road, London NW5 3HR

ISBN 1 85425 033 7

2 3 4 5 6 7 8 9 10 :: 99 98 97 96 95 94 93 92 91 90

Phototypeset by Input Typesetting, London

Printed in England by Biddles Ltd., Guildford, Surrey
on recycled paper

To Linda: a special lady.

To Kerry and Gareth – and their future.

Acknowledgements

I would like to thank those members of the Green Party and the pressure groups and organisations specialising in every field who read the manuscript and offered their excellent and valued observations.

Thanks also to Linda for putting up with me spending every spare moment throughout a whole summer shut away in the spare room, researching or writing. Her support, as always, was total.

And a big thanks to Jan Peters for typing the final draft with her usual enthusiasm and expertise.

Contents

Thoughts for Today

Every 24 hours an area of tropical forest the size of the Isle of Wight is destroyed or degraded; deserts advance by a similar area; 200 million tonnes of top soil is lost through erosion; at least one species becomes extinct; and 100,000 people, nearly half of them children, die through hunger. Every day.

Earthrights

But . . .

When, from the depths of our hearts, we desire something more real than material power, the wave of destruction will recede. Thence peace will come, joy will come, light will come.

Anon

Foreword

The man who has written this book is completely out of his mind. Quite bonkers.

Do you know he actually believes that you can't go on taking more and more from the Earth every year and turning it into more and more pollution. What nonsense!

Of course you can. We've always done it haven't we?

He says that if you destroy the base on which all life depends then you naturally destroy all life in the process. If that were true it would be mentioned in our manifestos and company reports – and it isn't, is it?

Honestly, who are these people? They say we can't have more growth on top of growth year after year or we will destroy ourselves. We think they must be a bit funny, you know. It's obvious what we need. More production means more money. Expansion, that's the only key to the good life.

So we advise you to read no further. The man is a dreamer. Thank goodness WE still live in the real world.

The author would like to thank the Conservative Party, the Labour Party, the Liberal Democrats, the Social Democrats, the Communist Party, every other major political movement around the world, and the global industrial system for their help in compiling this Foreword.

The Earth

If the Earth were only a few feet in diameter, floating a few feet above a field somewhere, people would come from everywhere to marvel at it.

People would walk around it, marvelling at its big pools of water, its little pools and the water flowing between the pools. People would marvel at the bumps on it, and the holes in it, and they would marvel at the very thin layer of gas surrounding it and the water suspended in the gas.

The people would marvel at all the creatures walking around the surface of the ball, and at the creatures in the water. The people would declare it sacred because it was the only one, and they would protect it so that it would not be hurt.

The ball would be the greatest wonder known, and the people would come to pray to it, to be healed, to gain knowledge, to know beauty and to wonder how it could be.

People would love it and defend it with their lives, because they would somehow know that their lives, their own roundness, could be nothing without it.

If the Earth were only a few feet in diameter.

Introduction

When I joined the Green Party we did not even register in most opinion polls. We were lumped together with the Monster Raving Loonies under 'others'.

When we launched the Isle of Wight Green Party there were fewer than ten members out of a population of more than 120,000. Two of those were my wife and me.

It was, therefore, an indication of the rise in our support that a member of the Labour Party actually told me I had only joined the Greens because I wanted to be an MP! What we are seeing is a new dawn in human awareness of our links with the rest of creation. It began with the explosion in the membership of environmental pressure groups and has now shown itself at the ballot box. A quiet, peaceful revolution is going on within millions of people, a revolution of values. Our children's future may yet be secured.

It is clear that a new force is gathering pace and threatens to sweep through the grey political establishment throughout the world. Their cosy game is in trouble. Sanity is breaking out.

Decade after decade they have knocked on our doors and told us whatever we wanted to hear: 'You want to get richer and richer every year? Then we are the party for you.' They never mention the consequences for the future of this irresponsible vote-catching. As long as we put our cross in the right place, that's all that really matters. 'The future? We'll face that when it comes.' Or someone else will.

You won't get this from the Greens. There is no point in trying to kid our way to Westminster by selling a fantasy. That doesn't win you power, it wins you office, the right to administer the system of destruction for another five years. The only power worth having is that secured by telling the truth, so that you have the support to do what really needs doing. If we go up to 50 per cent in the polls or down to 0.5 per cent, we will still be saying the same things because they are the truth.

As Fritz Schumacher put it so well:

> We must do what we conceive to be right and not bother our heads or burden our souls with whether we'll be successful.
> Because if we don't do the right thing, we'll do the wrong thing, and we'll be part of the disease and not part of the cure.

This is why the party has never compromised its principles and values to match the public climate of the time. Our values are not for sale because the future is not for sale. Today, at last, that climate is moving our way as the wisdom of the Green approach becomes ever clearer. Honesty and popularity need no longer stand alone.

People are realising, as all of us in the Green Party do, that the line we have been sold by the conventional politicians throughout our lives has led us down a highly dangerous and potentially fatal path. Yet now the parties around the world whose policies have caused the crisis and who said there would be no crisis, are asking us to believe they are the ones to get us out of the crisis. They even condemn the Green Party who predicted it all long ago as 'loony'.

If someone drives a car into a ditch because they don't know what they're doing, you don't send them off to drive the breakdown lorry. Conventional politics cannot be green. The two are a contradiction.

The word *green* is the most abused and misused in the English language. Changing to unleaded petrol is said to be 'going green', anything even vaguely associated with the environment is said to be a 'green issue', any politician at the Department of the Environment is said to be a 'green minister', even though their record may be shocking. I can understand why – it's a perfect word for a headline writer – but its use has become terribly misleading.

Green in the political sense means far more than most people realise. It is a vast concept that includes environmental protection, fundamental social justice, and values of non-violence, caring and sharing, and respect for all life on Earth. It includes all of those things because, as you will see, they are indivisible. The Westminster politicians should know that you can't be truly Green *if*:

• You support a system of economic growth achieved by giving more and more to the rich at the expense of the poor, the planet and future generations. In other words the present system.

• You believe it's possible to grow forever within a finite area and bombard fragile life support processes without destroying them and everything else.

• You continue to ignore the dangers arising from the world's exploding population and the need to address them in a responsible fashion.

• You see life in such narrow terms that you believe people should be grateful to have a 'job', even though it is mind-numbing, soul-destroying, and they hate every minute of it.

• You believe that giving everyone the chance to develop their natural talents and creativity with a new approach to work is 'idealism'.

• You think democracy is merely allowing people to vote every four or five years with no say in what happens in between.

• You allow property speculators to amass enormous wealth while people sleep in the streets and go hungry.

• You think it's fine for this country to import food from hungry nations to feed our livestock; you sanction the abuse of animals in factory farms on the grounds that it is 'economic';

or you support animal experimentation for which there is no moral or scientific justification whatsoever.

• You support the possession of nuclear weapons when the 'defence' argument for them is a delusion; or you encourage poor countries, often run by evil regimes, to buy your weapons at the expense of the hungry.

And that's just for starters.

Greens do not judge anyone by race, creed or colour, or by any other criteria, except by what they are as people. Greens seek to promote the gentler side of the character which everyone possesses. They believe in personal self-reliance and economic policies that reduce dependency on outside influences. Only then can people be free to control their own destiny. Greens offer a new economics which will improve the *quality* of life while protecting the *future* of life.

Green politics is about eliminating the cause of a problem, not just treating the symptoms. This is why the establishment parties and the powerful interest groups are so afraid of our essage. It is good to be 'green' – but only if you don't rock the boat too much or challenge the power of those who prosper from environmental and human exploitation. One Brazilian church leader highlighted this attitude when he said of his country's government:

> Why is it that when I give help to the poor they call me a saint, but when I ask *why* they are poor in the first place, they call me a communist?

So it is with Green politics. It is OK for us to be concerned about what is happening, but not for us to take action that might affect business as usual. You will appreciate already, I hope, that we are not a one-issue party. We can't be if we are to secure the future.

The range of Green Party policy covers all issues. In the

manifesto you will find policies on economics, employment and industry, health, education, foreign policy, overseas aid and development, social welfare, transport, public administration and government, human rights and civil liberties, taxation, decentralisation, defence, agriculture, energy, food, animal rights ... etc ... etc ... plus, naturally, our comprehensive range of directly environmental policies.

All that policy isn't there for the sake of it. All human and economic activity affects the environment, or is itself affected by environmental degradation. If you don't acknowledge that in *all* your policies, you can't begin to solve the immense problems we face.

Green politics is not just about tightening up the planning laws, though that's important. It's not just about saving a meadow here or a species there, though that's very important as well. Green politics is much more than that – because unless you get to the cause of environmental destruction, then while you are trying to save this meadow or that species, other meadows and other species are disappearing all around you. It's the cause we have to address and the cause is the dream world we are living in, spending our children's future and their children's future.

Green values demand justice for all. Injustice, the domination of some people over others, is at the core of our environmental and social problems. An unfair society is a doomed society. You can't tell people they must consume less when their children are hungry. You can't tell a family in some rotting council flat or a bed and breakfast slum that they are living beyond the the means of nature to support them. You can't tell the Brazilian poor that they must stop cutting down trees when they have to survive another day. And you can't tell those skin and bones they call children in Ethiopia and elsewhere that they must stop abusing the planet.

We, the fortunate people, must consume less so they can consume more.

In these pages I will outline the Green vision of a human race that lives in harmony with the planet; of a country and a world that put the needs of all peoples before the wants of the few.

I hope I can help you to appreciate the causes of our environmental and social problems. Those causes are kept hidden from most of us throughout our lives because it suits powerful vested interests to stop the truth coming out. To present you with this truth, I have naturally had to look in some detail at the problems we face and why they are getting worse. However, I want to stress most strongly before we start that the answers are there, often staring us in the face.

When you read of this destruction or that human misery, don't let it sap your spirit or make you turn away and think, 'There's nothing we can do, so why bother?' It's not true. I can't imagine a better way to sum up Green politics than in the line: *It doesn't have to be like this*. It really doesn't. Yes, the problems are many and serious, and yes, we don't have limitless time to sort them out, but it can be done, and it will be done if the Greens are given the chance.

I will keep repeating this message because it is vital that we recognise that the human race need not be overwhelmed by its own folly. No one can turn it all around in a short time; it's going to be a long haul, but we can stop much of it getting worse relatively quickly if we are determined enough and united enough.

Green politics is about hope and vision. Not despair.

David Icke
Ryde, 1989

1: From Grey to Green

We face a future daily becoming more frightening: a future of increasing conflict, accelerating misery and poverty; of one-upmanship, and winners and losers. It's a future we can still change – but we need to start now.

Green Politics are today's politics as well as tomorrow's.
GREEN PARTY ELECTION MANIFESTO 1987

Well what a turn-up. From professional footballer to television presenter to green politician. Whatever next?

Nothing next.

There is nothing I could possibly do that is more important, more urgent, than campaign for Green values at the heart of politics. What is left of my life will be dedicated to that end.

It all started for me around the age of 13 in my home city of Leicester. I lived on a big council estate and I used to go out into the countryside on my bike. It was one of the great joys of my childhood. Over time I began to notice areas that were once beautiful countryside disappearing under concrete and I remember standing there one day while the bulldozers had their way again thinking 'This can't go on for ever – there'll be nothing left.'

Now here I am all these years later doing everything I can to promote a political philosophy that is based on that same simple truth. That nothing can go on growing forever without destroying itself, a simple truth the other parties refuse to see. So I was aware of the impact humans were having from that early age, but it was a long time before I realised just how massive and potentially lethal that impact could be.

I received a leaflet through the post from Greenpeace. I was stunned. It was called *Paradise Lost, Countdown to Destruction* and it said this:

> Planet Earth is 4,600 million years old. If we condense this inconceivable timespan into an understandable concept, we can liken the Earth to a person of 46 years of age.
>
> Nothing is known about the first seven years of this person's life, and whilst only scattered information exists about the middle span, we know that only at the age of 42 did the Earth begin to flower.
>
> Dinosaurs and the great reptiles did not appear until a year ago when the planet was 45. Mammals arrived only eight months ago and in the middle of last week men-like apes evolved into ape-like men, and at the weekend the last ice-age enveloped the Earth.
>
> Modern Man has been around for four hours. During the last hour Man discovered agriculture. The industrial revolution began a minute ago and during those 60 seconds of biological time man has made a rubbish tip of a paradise. He has multiplied his numbers to plague proportions, caused the extinction of 500 species of animals, ransacked the Planet for fuels and now stands like a brutish infant, gloating over his meteoric rise to ascendency, on the brink of a war to end all wars and of effectively destroying this oasis of life in the solar system.

In the few seconds it took to read, everything changed. We all go through life with the blinkers on, with tunnel vision, consumed by our own little world. That's understandable because we are bound to concentrate on the things that directly affect us. But once you get the chance to step back and survey the whole picture, the consequences of five billion little worlds on the Earth today, you are never the same again.

Once I'd read that leaflet my transition began – from being an environmentalist to being Green. There is a big difference between the two. An environmentalist believes you can protect the Earth within the present economic order. A Green says that's impossible, because it is the economic order that is the cause of all the trouble.

I joined as many pressure groups as I could and eventually the old Liberal Party – because their manifesto said they would defend the environment. I was later to learn the truth. It became clear that when viewed from within they were just like everyone else, blindly supporting the system of destruction without a second thought.

My concern for environmental issues was seen as a bit eccentric and over the top when there were so many more important issues to think about, like how to get more industry whatever the cost, more expansion, more economic growth. I was on the short list of four for the Isle of Wight parliamentary seat when I could take no more. What was the point of becoming an MP for the sake of it if my party was so at odds with the way I felt? I stood down.

I left the Liberal Party in some despair, and I thought that was the end of politics. Maybe it was me, maybe I was taking environmental problems too seriously, but on the evidence surely not. With the help of some committed environmentalists, I started a pressure group called Islandwatch which campaigns for sane planning on the Isle of Wight and the preservation of character, beauty and wildlife habitat. It works well and has earned respect from everyone except those who wish to sweep the concrete carpet across the Island and everywhere else. But it was soon obvious to me that the answers had to be political.

Pressure groups do a magnificent job and without their energy and effort we would be even closer to the edge. But they are not the answer in themselves. They can't be. They are always going to be engaged in a process of damage limitation, for reasons that will become clear. They are dealing mostly with the results of environmental damage when we must also address the cause – and the cause is political and economic.

It was at this point that I wrote to the Green Party and asked for their manifesto. This was the second document to change my life. The first had alerted me to the scale of the problem; now before me were many of the answers. Here was a political party that was not prepared to tell people what they wanted to hear if that was at odds with the truth. Here was a party not only prepared, but determined, to face the realities the others shied away from, didn't appreciate, or simply ignored.

Hallelujah!

I started the Isle of Wight Green Party with Linda and within two weeks the local Liberal Party, or the SLD as it became, was ordering a ban on CFC aerosols in council-run buildings – years after they knew the consequences of CFCs for the ozone layer! To those who believe they can change their own parties from within, all I can say is that my experience shows that parties respond to pressures from outside far more than they do from inside. On the inside you are just a niggling irritant they have to humour or put up with. On the outside you can cost them votes. To a traditional politician that is a fundamental difference.

Chico Mendes, the leader of the Brazilian Rubber Tappers, who was murdered for trying to protect the rainforests, also saw the reality of this. Two weeks before he died in 1988, he described traditional party policies as a 'tragic, ridiculous, system'.

He said of the so-called parties of the people:

Without realising it, workers are like the person who meets an injured lion, cures the lion and then gets eaten by it! The workers strengthen the politicians who then defend the workers' enemies. And many workers have still not discovered this.

One thing you see when you look at the world from the *truly green* perspective is that all the political movements – Conservatism, Socialism, Liberal Democracy, Communism – are all the same in their basic approach. They might see different ways of spending wealth and of taxing it, but they see the same way of creating it: by the ruthless exploitation of the natural world to the point of its destruction. In other words, more traditional growth every year.

Today capitalism, communism, and those in between blame each other while they all head for the same abyss. The environmental results of unbridled market forces can be seen throughout the West and the poor countries those forces exploit; while state control has, for its part, presented the Soviet Union with some of the worst devastation anywhere on Earth. Large areas of Eastern Europe are little more than wastelands, ecological cemeteries. No wonder we refer to these people collectively as the *grey* parties, the parties of yesterday with no solutions to offer to the great challenges we face in our battle for the planet.

The Green political movement is now growing to span the World it is dedicated to protect. It has been a hard road. Being honest and responsible, refusing to avoid the truth just to win votes, is not easy when the others have no such scruples. But we have stuck by our principles and refused to wilt whatever the scale of scorn and derision. Now as the Earth cries out for mercy, people are listening and they are joining us like never before. We are setting the agenda and we will continue to do so because the Earth will demand it. The world will have a green future or no future.

There was something else in that Greenpeace leaflet I have never forgotten. The Greenpeace ship, the Rainbow Warrior, so bravely bombed by the French in Auckland Harbour, got its name from an ancient Red Indian legend which was quite mind-blowing in its prophecy:

When the Earth is sick and the animals have disappeared, there
will come a tribe of people from all creeds, colours and
cultures, who believe in deeds not words and who will restore

the Earth to its former beauty. This tribe will be called the Warriors of the Rainbow.

One warrior reporting for duty. For life.

2: The suicide note

We are now faced with the fact that tomorrow is today. There is such a thing as being too late. Over the bleached bones of numerous civilisations are written the pathetic words: 'Too late'. If we do not act, we shall surely be dragged down the dark corridors of time reserved for those who possess power without compassion, might without morality and strength without sight.

MARTIN LUTHER KING

The perfect assassin

Here lies the body of Planet Earth. Cause of death? Human illusion.

Hardly a fitting tribute to the greatest gift in all creation, but it will be true all the same if we go on as we are. Illusion – that's what's killing the Earth.

It is the illusion promoted by all the political parties – the Green Party uniquely apart – and by the whole Western-style, Eastern-bloc-style, economic system that has been imposed on the World. Thousands of millions of people have been programmed from cradle to grave to believe it, too. It is the illusion that you can go on having more unquestioned economic growth on top of growth year after year; that you can go on expanding, expanding, exploiting, exploiting, polluting, polluting, on and on for ever and ever without destroying the very planet, the very natural world that we need to maintain life on Earth.

The Earth is finite, but the system sees only infinity. That's the fact the politicians in Westminster and elsewhere have refused to face.

As we have seen, the system has wreaked its destruction with staggering speed. It has taken the Earth 4,600 million years to evolve, yet the industrial system has been with us for less than 200. Much of the most serious destruction has happened in the last 40 years. The Industrial Revolution was a change in human activity unprecedented in history and it has brought about an equally unprecedented threat to life on Earth.

What we are seeing, as the Green Party predicted long ago, is the insane pursuit of unlimited, uncontrolled, uncaring growth colliding with the limits of nature to survive the punishment. It is a live now, pay later system. We live now, our children pay later. We live today by destroying tomorrow.

All this happens because modern economics are not designed to meet the needs of people or the planet. They are designed for one thing alone: throughput.

For 200 years we have been sitting on a suicidal conveyor belt that has got faster and faster with every passing decade. It devours the Earth's resources as fast as it can, the faster it takes them the more successful it is said to be. The faster it takes them the bigger the so called 'economic boom'. It then turns these irreplaceable resources into 'things', the vast majority of which we don't need. But the advertising industry spends billions of pounds a year persuading us we do need them, or at least we want them, or we are not whole, complete, successful human beings unless we have them. These 'things' are not made to last, as they could be, because the system needs us to buy them again and again, and every year the aim of every economy has been to take more from the Earth even quicker, make even more things, sell even more things, to worship the god called economic growth.

It is take, make and throw away . . . take, make and throw away . . . that's why the system is devastating the Earth. It can't help it. It is the perfect assassin.

I ask you, what kind of economics is it that damages the Earth quicker when it's successful and damages it more slowly when it's in recession? Arthur Daley governments with Arthur

Daley values have encouraged this like never before in recent times. They follow the old cowboy motto of shoot first, ask questions later. But later is always too late. It is they who have encouraged people to base their decisions and political preference on 'What's in it for me?'

Green economics, as you will see, are designed to reduce throughput to a comparative trickle so that eventually we will not be taking more from the Earth than it can naturally replenish. This, in turn, will have a dramatic effect on pollution. The slower the throughput, the less pollution created. What's more, this can be done while at the same time reducing hunger, poverty and human misery. It sounds idealistic and I plead 'guilty' there. It is more than that, though. It is possible.

The system

I will be referring many times to 'the system' and so I should offer a definition at this early stage. By the system I mean a form of economic thinking that sees the profit figure at the bottom of the balance sheet every year as the only measurement of success. Keeping the shareholders happy and increasing profits by the biggest margin possible is its only aim in life. The effects on people and the planet of the processes needed to produce those maximum profits are way down the list of priorities, if indeed they are taken into account at all. The system also includes the government and military machine and most of the media which support and promote either directly or indirectly the 'wisdom' of these mixed up and misguided economic principles. And the system most certainly includes the advertising industry which aims to seduce us to earn, earn, earn and spend, spend, spend to fuel the ever increasing throughput on which the whole house of cards depends. It is all short-term and short-sighted.

I have heard it said that the real problem is a crisis of human values, of the way we see the world and how we judge what is truly important and successful. This is quite right. But what shapes human values? What has control of the messages we receive throughout our lives? What gives us the 'facts' it wants us to know, but not the facts it doesn't, so that our opinions and values are shaped by wrong or limited information? What sets out the criteria by which people are considered 'successful'? Answer: the system.

It is true that some of us have been fortunate enough to see through it all because we have read the right books and met the right people and the emergence of a strong Green movement is making this easier, but most people still get their information from the voices of the system and this has an enormous impact on the way they think and react. It was the same with me before I stumbled on the truth some years ago.

Whenever I have asked how the system I've described can possibly operate without inevitably destroying the planet, no one has been able to answer me. Whenever I ask that question there is always silence, a shrug of the shoulders maybe, but always silence or at most 'It can't, but . . .' It can't, but nothing.

But the grey parties still try to tell us it can. They have always promoted and supported the impossible dream, that growth as currently measured can go on for ever and, astonishingly, against all the evidence now before us, they still believe it. They persuade others to believe it, too; that is the tragedy. Most people buy this line because that's what they have always been told throughout their lives – so it must be true. They also have families to bring up, livings to earn, lives to lead and they don't have time to study politics or read books that will give them the facts the politicians and advertisers are keeping from them. This makes it much easier for politicians and the system in general to manipulate them and sell them their illusions.

The system has become so complex it is almost impossible for people to follow, and deep down there is still this belief, despite what some might say, that our leaders would not be misguided enough to lead us to disaster. 'If what you say is true, they would do something about it,' I have been told on several occasions. The world *is* complex and that muddies the waters. It becomes a nightmare trying to make sense of it all, so 'experts' and politicians can go on television talking confidently in language we often don't understand. They tell us black is white and we get terribly confused.

The Green alternative

When you strip down the system, discard all the cosmetics and complications, you see that it is the longest suicide note in history. Indeed, if you look at the age of the planet against the timescale of destruction, it could even be the shortest suicide note in history, yet only the Green Parties and genuine Green thinkers of the world are trying to expose it, discredit it, replace it.

First rule of green politics, *truly* green politics: you cannot divorce the economic system and human values from the destruction of the planet. You can't because one causes the other. You can't have uncontrolled market forces and indiscriminate economic expansion, you can't have free-for-all consumerism and shockingly wasteful energy policies and protect the planet, you simply can't.

Yet the grey parties are all agreed that we must have more economic growth to create the wealth to protect the environment. If you are indoctrinated by the system that can actually make sense. In reality it is nonsense.

What they can't see is that the more economic growth of the traditional kind you have, the more you damage the environment. They are saying we must create more wealth to pay for repairing damage (where possible) that is caused by the process of creating more wealth. As one of our German colleagues put it so well, that policy is merely trying to clean the teeth of the dragon when it is the dragon itself, the system, that has to be tamed. What the grey parties are saying is that the way to put out the fire is to pour more petrol on it.

Jonathon Porritt got it right in his book, *Seeing Green*, when he said the traditional parties are like cars on a motorway, in different lanes maybe and travelling at different speeds, but all going in the same direction. The Green Party is another direction. It knows an illusion when it sees one.

If we are to stop the devastation, we must accept the reality that we are living well beyond the means of nature to support the way we live. We have so lost touch with the natural world that we have been deluded into believing that we are somehow above nature, superior to it. We are not, we are part of it, a strand in the web of life and if we destroy enough strands, we destroy ourselves. The system in its arrogance has set out to control nature, to bludgeon it into submission so it can be master. The problem is that the world doesn't work like that, as we are learning to our cost.

It is easy to see why we have lost our links with nature. Eighty per cent of people in this country live in towns and cities, surrounded by the products of human activity. The race is on to turn every remaining open space into a 'development' that makes the developer richer and the community invariably poorer. They call it infilling. Whatever they call it, our links with nature, increasingly tenuous since the dawn of the industrial revolution, have been lost altogether in many of our bleak, urban landscapes. No wonder we have taken nature for granted for so long.

The web of life

If we don't appreciate the interdependence between the natural world and our part within it, we play a very dangerous game. If you poison the sea bed – as we do – with sewage sludge dumping, chemicals and radioactive waste, the poison is picked up by the minute organisms which are eaten by the fish and other sea life. They, in turn, are eaten by humans. The poisons may have settled on the sea bed, but they still end up on your dinner plate.

Rainforests are another superb example of this interdependency. For 30 million years they have produced the most lush vegetation on Earth. Up to the 1950s they were still relatively intact. By the end of the century at current rates of depletion there will be little left.

This lush vegetation makes many think the soil must be very fertile, ideal for crops. But this fertility comes from the dead, rotting, trees and plants which, in the hot, moist climate, break down very quickly releasing their nutrients for the living plants and trees to take up.

So when you cut down the vegetation, you take away the source of the fertility and very soon the soil is useless semi-desert. What's more, with the forest gone the climate changes and there is less rain. This is how the rainforests, one of the wonders of the world, are turned into barren wasteland to 'graze' cattle for western hamburgers or to provide massive profits for multi-national corporations through timber and mineral exploitation.

Like all of nature, the rainforests live and thrive in a cycle in which one thing provides for another until you get back to the beginning again. It could go on like that indefinitely if it were not that humans are breaking these cycles, these eco-systems, every minute of every year throughout the world, to live in a way the planet cannot support.

You could say the Earth was giving us £100 a week to spend and that would be OK, it could cope with that. But we are spending £150. To make up the difference we are dipping into our capital, nature in all its forms, the processes we need to keep us alive and well, now and in the future.

Who pays the cost?

We are not paying the true cost of what we produce and what we consume, but our children will – and the people of the poor world already are. Much of what we buy is only 'economic' because that real cost is not being paid. Instead of disposing of our waste safely or avoiding dangerous processes, we pour our poisons into the rivers, the seas, and the air because that's cheaper. The planet is used as little more than a limitless source of resources at one end of the production line and a free dustbin at the other. This way their products are 'economic' in the short term, but they are destroying the future.

It is a system that is supposed to provide for everyone, but its values and aims are so perverted that while it can pay a businessman a million pounds a year, it leaves others, often youngsters fresh out of school, to sleep in a box in the street. And to enable us, the pampered few, to have our choices and luxuries, men, women and children thousands of miles away have to suffer hunger, misery and starvation beyond human comprehension – as I will be explaining.

It reacts only to 'demand' which means the demands of those who can afford to buy. This way the system only produces for those who have plenty and not for those who have nothing. If you don't have the money to stimulate 'demand' for what you need, I'm afraid you don't exist in the throughput mentality.

The whole crazy system is only made possible by the ruthless exploitation of the Earth's resources, the dismantling of our own life support processes, and the criminal, inhuman exploitation of the poorest and weakest peoples in the world. It is geologically and ecologically unsustainable and morally unjustifiable. It cannot go on.

What we need are the values, the commonsense and responsibility of Green economics which can see the difference between wants and needs. The true needs of all people should be met, can be met, while the wants must be limited by what the planet can stand, not by what the markets will take.

As Gandhi said: 'The Earth has enough for everyone's need, but not for everyone's greed.'

The politics of more and more have got us into this mess, the politics of enough for all, Green politics, must get us out of it.

Tackling the causes

We are the Symptom Society. Our politicians (when pressed by public opinion and the thought of lost votes) will agree to treat the symptoms of a problem, but not the cause. The Green Party will replace this obsession with symptoms and address causes and – another key word – *connections*. This means looking in detail at how any course of action affects people and the planet. So much damage and misery is the result of these connections being ignored or hidden from us.

Our values have become warped and degraded by the system and those who do its bidding, be they politicians, top civil servants, industrial leaders or advertising copy writers. Our economics are so out of touch with the rest of creation that to produce our food they pour chemicals on to the land, polluting the air and water supplies, killing wildlife and over a period even poisoning the very people they feed.

To produce our meat such economics insists that farm animals are treated with terrible cruelty, given growth inducers and antibiotics, the consequences of which for human health no one can tell.

And to produce our poultry and eggs 'economically', our chickens are kept in conditions that can only be described as evil. They live their whole wretched lives being kidded that night is day and day is night in an area not much bigger than this piece of paper.

Human victims

Animals and the planet are not the only victims. Our economics degrades people, too. To the system we are not human beings with feelings and emotions and aspirations. We are mere units of production and consumption. Our only rôle is to produce things that other people can consume so we can earn money to consume the things the other people produce. It means that millions do jobs they hate so they can buy things they don't really need over and over again.

The Harvard Business Review did a survey among the heads of the biggest corporations which revealed the true power of advertising. Eighty-five per cent said that advertising 'frequently' persuades people to buy things for which they have no use, and more than half said that advertising persuades people to buy things they don't really want!

The system scars and enslaves our very souls.

Contentment is not to *have* more and more and more, contentment is not to *want* more and more and more. But the advertising industry, the bellows of the system, spends its billions, sharpens up its psychology, to make us want, to make us chase the dream that more possessions mean more happiness. The system spends its fortunes buying our contentment; the consequences are all around us in unhappiness, crime, aggression, violence, despair, mental breakdown, family break-up and endless other social and human problems.

What else do we expect in a world that sees a land speculator as successful because he makes a pile from it, while someone doing a vital job on a small wage is somehow a failure by comparison. What do we expect when people are judged not by what they *are*, but by what they *own*?

There is such a difference between being clever and being wise. The system is very clever. Every year it invents new things to make, new ways of making them, ever more sophisticated ways of selling them. Yes, it's clever. But it isn't wise enough to see the consequences of what it does, nor is it wise enough, perhaps, even to care.

As we are now learning every day, cleverness without wisdom is the most destructive force on Earth.

3: The growth obsession

> What becomes a man if the process of production takes away
> from work any hint of humanity, making of it a merely
> mechanical activity. The worker himself is turned into a
> perversion of a free being.
>
> And so bodily labour (said Pius XI) which even after
> original sin was decreed by Providence for the good of man's
> body and soul, is in many instances changed into an
> instrument of perversion; for from the factory, dead matter
> goes out improved, whereas people are corrupted and
> degraded.
>
> E. F. SCHUMACHER: *SMALL IS BEAUTIFUL*

The theory is that the more 'things' you make and the more
'things' you sell, the more people are employed and the better
off everyone will be.

So expand the production of 'things' – whatever they may
be – and as long as you can get people to buy them all will be
well, because it will mean lots of economic growth. That's the
grey party, grey economic theory that dominates our system.

That's the theory. Now the reality.

The system sees the economic growth figure as the measurement of national wellbeing. You hear chancellors proclaiming in
budget speeches how their wonderful handling of the country's
finances has meant 'unprecedented levels of economic growth'.

The backbenchers cheer with uncontrollable glee and the
opposition parties squabble over whose policies will produce
more growth. If everyone is so obsessed with this growth, why
is the Green Party so fundamentally opposed to it in its present
form?

Stone age economics

Economic policy based on increasing the Gross National Product is the economics of the Stone Age. It is not a guide to national wellbeing. It is hardly a guide to anything. It measures only the amount of money that has changed hands for goods and services in the economy. Not who spends it or what on; not how the money was made; not the environmental and human costs of making and spending that money; not the loss of finite resources involved.

For politicians and economists to stand up day after day using this 'growth' as the answer to all economic and social ills is shocking and thoroughly misleading. Let us look at some examples of this measurement of national economic wellbeing.

Say an oil tanker went aground off the British coast and poured its contents into the sea. It would cause environmental devastation of the kind we saw in Prince William Sound in Alaska. Bird and marine life would take decades to recover, if indeed they ever did.

Now apply the yardstick of economic growth to such a disaster. The money paid to the tanker company for the original journey would be added to economic growth. So would the money paid in insurance for the loss of the ship and the oil. And the money paid to the people who salvaged the ship. And the money spent on medical services and the helicopter company to fly the injured to hospital. And the money spent by the organisations trying to save the wildlife. The list goes on and on.

All this is added to the figure of national economic wellbeing. Our system turns an environmental disaster into an economic growth bonanza. We say that's a nonsense. Who's crazy, us or them?

Every time there is a road accident it adds to economic growth; the worse the accident, the more the growth. Every time someone is ill and needs treatment, that adds to economic growth. The more serious the illness, the more the treatment, the more the growth. Our system counts them all as positive.

So if the Green Party reduced road accidents, illness, environmental damage and all the rest, as our policies would, then economic growth would fall. Would that be a bad thing? Quite the opposite.

Every time we take finite resources from the Earth we are adding to economic growth. So if the Green Party ensured through true efficiency and responsible economic policies that we dramatically reduced our use of irreplaceable resources, the economic growth would fall. But would that be a bad thing? Quite the opposite.

The annual growth figure takes both the economic expansion and the environmental and human costs of that expansion and adds them all together. This makes it impossible to work out how much we are benefitting from growth, if at all, and at what cost. The figure the politicians worship is, in fact, meaningless.

The hidden costs of 'growth'

What we should be doing is subtracting all the costs of expansion from the benefits to find out how much progress is really being made. This the Green Party would do by replacing the Gross National Product with an Adjusted National Product. What a shock this would produce. It would reveal that a substantial amount of our economic growth actually costs us as much or more wealth than it creates. It is a bit like spending £5.50 to visit someone with the intention of borrowing a fiver. This has never been revealed before because the present system does not take into account damage to the environment, the waste of finite resources, and the many costs and consequences of replacing people with machines to increase growth.

The Green approach takes a much wider view of efficiency than merely how low individual companies can keep their costs and how high they can keep their profits. When you take away all the hidden costs of growth which are paid for by the community in pollution and other environmental damage, ill-health, unemployment, road building and repairs, road accidents, and so on, you see the conventional view of efficiency in a very different light. These past 200 years the system has ignored such costs and passed many of them on to future generations, but they are all coming back to haunt us. The environmental bailiffs are at the door.

Greens believe economic wellbeing should be judged by more relevant measurements – like how many people are hungry or homeless or ill, and how many are unfulfilled, under stress, and yes, unhappy. The growth obsession is not the answer to these problems, it's the cause. There would be new measurements of success in industry. For instance, we would not judge the fishing industry simply on how many fish they catch. The crucial figure would be how many are left in the sea. Is it more or less than last year?

A cruder measure of economic success than growth you could not contrive. It wasn't meant to be used in this way. It was meant to be just one of a number of measurements to see how well the country was doing. Instead it has become the figure followed blindly by politicians, economists, industry, and the whole system East and West. The growth obsession is devouring the Earth.

You see, we're not just talking about growth, but growth on top of growth. Say you start at one and have a three per cent growth rate in the first year which under the present system would be considered only fair. In the second year, if you have another growth rate of three per cent, that is not three per cent on top of the starting figure of one. It is three per cent on top of last year's three per cent. In two years you are already producing and consuming six per cent more than when you started.

Under this system to maintain that three per cent growth rate every year we have to *double* what we produce and consume in 25 years! A three per cent growth rate over 200 years means that in 200 years time we will have to produce and consume more in a *day* than we are currently doing in a *year*.

When you look at the health of the Earth now, you see that if we go on at that rate we haven't got anything like 200 years before the damage is irreparable. It's nearer 50 years. In the way we measure it today, it's not a choice between growth or no growth. It's between no growth and no life.

Do we want quantity or quality? We complain about air pollution, traffic jams, the loss of countryside, yet, as Walter Schwarz pointed out in his demolition of growth in *The Guardian*:

> Every percentage point of economic growth adds hundreds of
> thousands of centrally heated homes, and cars, more
> supermarkets and washing machines, more roads, more acres
> of fields under concrete.
>
> To maintain growth we need to sell to the Third World so
> that it, too, can grow. China, which contributes nine per cent
> of the world's carbon dioxide through its coal burning, expects
> its energy demand in the year 2030 to be six times what it was
> in 1980. India and Brazil with faster growing populations have
> comparable hopes . . .
>
> . . . The gleaming bathroom and kitchen, the well-stocked
> refrigerator, his and her cars in the drive: for half a century
> that stereotyped model of well-being has been flashed across
> cinema screens from Tibet to Timbuktu. It is a dream, a religion
> that has been far more effective at converting than Christianity.
> Disillusion is at hand: there will be six billion people by 1998
> and they cannot live like that.

And what are we doing it for? To give everyone a decent standard of living? Hardly. Not when the few can get fabulously wealthy by abusing the Earth while others sleep in the streets, live in misery, or die for the want of food in a world (for the moment) of plenty.

The poverty of growth and the growth of poverty

In the United States, which has had fantastic growth since the war, there is enormous poverty. There has been growth in poor countries while their people have gone hungry. This is because it's the wrong kind of growth and the wrong kind of development. The Americans have used more fossil fuels and minerals in the last 50 years than all the other countries in the world in the whole of human history. If growth is the way to eliminate poverty then why haven't the Americans managed it – despite consuming the Earth on this suicidal scale? And what would be left if every country did the same, including those in the Third World? Yet that is what they have been told to do. It's madness.

Growth of the present kind makes the rich richer at the expense of the poor in this country and around the world – and at the expense of our children and the future.

The world has had a century of economic growth and yet half the population of the planet is in relative or absolute poverty – 800 million are in absolute poverty, the definition of which is 'a condition of life so characterised by malnutrition, illiteracy, and disease as to be beneath any reasonable definition of human decency.' The situation is getting worse and will continue to get worse until even the richest few are affected by the depletion of the natural base on which all life depends.

This is why the blind pursuit of more and more is leading to less and less – and eventually nothing – for everyone.

There is no such thing as human-made wealth because it all derives from the Earth. We have lost sight of the fact that, in truth, all wealth comes from exploiting natural wealth; the source of all our prosperity is under enormous threat. As the saying goes: 'When you have cut down the last tree and polluted the last river, you will know that you cannot eat money'.

I never cease to wonder when I hear the voices of left-wing politics demanding more expansion and growth to provide for the poor. They could not be more wrong. The growth system, far from being able to eliminate poverty, actually *needs* poverty to survive. Firstly it needs to have the poor there as a constant reminder of what happens if you don't play by the rules, and crucially, it needs poverty to justify its further expansion. Indeed these very left-wing voices are helping it to do that.

The 'trickle-down' fallacy

When government ministers are asked about the poverty all around us despite a so-called boom, they tell us we must make our economy more efficient so we can compete on the world market and increase our growth rate. Then we can spend more on the poor, they say.

But look what happens. The economy is expanded and who gain most? Those at the top. Who gain least or not at all? Those at the bottom.

This is because the process of wealth distribution is, by design, so inefficient. It is called 'trickle down'. The idea is that if you allow some people or countries to get very rich then they will spend that money and some of it will 'trickle down' to poorer people and poorer countries. This theory tricks even caring politicians into seeing more expansion and growth as the way to help the poor. Unfortunately, it doesn't work – and look at the consequences for the planet.

Because the re-distribution is so bad, it means you have to create an astonishing amount of wealth for the few at the top for those at the bottom to get even the bare minimum to survive. Many don't even get that much which is why 100,000 die every day from hunger-related disease. Yet it is the process of creating that wealth at the top that is at the heart of our environmental crisis.

What we have to do is meet the needs of everyone while keeping within the limits set by nature. That doesn't mean more growth of the present kind, but more distribution and more true efficiency.

The guarantee of Basic Income

The Green Party would reduce the dependence on trickle down with a tax-free 'Basic Income' to cover basic needs for everyone whether they work or not. Tax allowances, pensions and most social security payments would be replaced by basic income paid to everyone, men, women and children. The highest payments would go to the disabled and those of current pension age, and the child's payment would go to the legal guardian as with child benefit.

It would not be a fortune, far from it, but it would cover basic living costs, to make sure no one has to be cold, hungry or homeless. Those on adequate incomes would receive their payment as a tax concession while the rest would receive it in cash.

The money would come from various sources. Basic Income would replace tax allowances and tax would be paid progressively the higher the income. The money for Basic Income would also come from that already spent today on other benefits and from our new Community Ground Rent. It is designed to discourage land speculation and to share the financial benefits of land ownership with the community as a whole. It is quite wrong that a tiny number of people who control large amounts of land should keep all advantages of that ownership for themselves. The higher the commercial rental value of the land, the higher the rent paid to the community, so farmers and growers would pay the least. Our reduction in arms spending would also free resources for Basic Income, and it would be phased in as the other changes were made and the finance became available.

Just think of the opportunities a guaranteed Basic Income would open up for people, even without the environmental case for ridding ourselves of the trickle down system. All the 'traps' would go for a start, like the unemployment and poverty traps.

The unemployment and poverty traps

The unemployment trap creates the ridiculous situation where on one side you have unemployed people who want to work and on the other you have work that needs doing for the good of the community. The problem is that you can't put the two together because the rate of pay for the work is less than you can get in benefits.

When you have a family to feed you are not going to take a job that pays you less than the benefit rate – which often leaves people in poverty as it is.

Under the Basic Income Scheme you could do that necessary work and the money would be added to your Basic Income, not taken away from it. This means you are contributing to your community, and your family's needs are provided for much better than now. Far from being a disincentive to work, like the present benefits system, Basic Income is the opposite. At the moment, you stay on the dole and the work stays undone. You are, in effect, paid not to work.

The poverty trap affects people who are in low paid work and have their income topped up by means-tested benefit. If your wage goes up a little, your benefits come down. You can work harder and end up with less. Talk about despair. What are people like that supposed to do?

With Basic Income that could not happen. The harder you worked the more you would earn. The days of the repulsive means test would be gone for ever and so would these and the other traps.

It would ease fear and insecurity because people would know that money was coming in every week no matter what and it would ensure that no one would go without the basics while, at the same time, being an incentive to work.

The Basic Income would be paid to self-employed people as well, the number of whom would rise substantially under the Green Party. It would give them more security and encouragement to set up new small businesses and help them through the lean spells. It would give women an independent income and recognise the value of the enormous amount of voluntary, unpaid, work that goes on without which the economy would collapse.

It would make it easier for people to take time off to study and re-train, whatever their age. It would allow people to work part-time and job share. This is important because the days of full-time, full employment, at least five days a week for everyone, are over. In fact, they were never here.

Periods of full employment have been few, brief, and did not count women. This pursuit of full-time, full employment through the trickle-down growth system has done so much to create the dragon. Yet still the illusion prevails. The present system can't rid us of unemployment. It is made up of too many contradictions. For instance, the more it tries to compete on the world market in the name of creating jobs, the more it turns to machinery for more 'efficient' production. So more jobs go.

Appropriate technology

The Green Party is most certainly not against technology. Many of the answers will come from it, but on the other hand so have most of our problems. Technology is not just kidney machines and premature baby units, it is nuclear power, nuclear weapons, lethal chemicals and soulless production lines. Technology can replace dangerous jobs and that is wonderful. But it can also replace work that should be quite properly done by human beings. That is far from wonderful and we would use the tax system to encourage the use of people.

The key word here and in every other aspect of green thinking is *appropriate*. The use of appropriate technology would be decided by its effect on people in the widest sense. Simply increasing one company's profits would not be justification in itself.

Appropriate technology is that which people use to support their own creativity, not that which replaces that creativity. Machine minding technology is not, then, appropriate. Nor is that which wastes natural resources or harms the environment either because of the pollution it produces or the damage caused in extracting the resources it needs. Today's mass production technology fails at every stage.

Green politics is not about going back, but forward to a new age in which science and technology are used for the benefit of people and the planet. We would use the knowledge human beings have gained this century and will go on gaining to create technology that is environmentally friendly and sees the needs of people as the point of its existence. The means to produce most of it already exists.

There are more scientists in the world today than in all of previous history, yet there are more problems today than ever before. I thought science is supposed to solve problems, but every 'solution' seems to produce yet more problems to solve. Thinking about it, that's probably why there are so many scientists! The so-called technological fix is often no more than a technological fixation.

It is not that science and technology are bad, but simply that they have been used in the wrong way. They have been used to destroy, not repair and protect, to alienate and replace people, not to support and develop them.

The Green Party's view of technology is summed up in Fritz Schumacher's visionary book, *Small is Beautiful:*

> Man cannot live without science and technology any more than he can live without nature. What needs careful consideration, however, is the *direction* of scientific research. We cannot leave that to the scientists alone . . . That direction should be towards non-violence rather violence: towards a harmonious co-operation with nature rather than a warfare against nature; towards the noiseless, low-energy, elegant, and economical

solutions normally applied in nature rather than the noisy, high-energy, brutal, wasteful, and clumsy solutions of our present day sciences.

The continuation of scientific advance in the direction of ever-increasing violence, culminating in nuclear fission . . . is a prospect threatening the abolition of Man.

Experience has shown that the direction of technological and scientific research and development can no longer be left to scientists and business people. They have ensured that the research and development has been fuelled only by the quest for ever lower costs (for them) and ever higher profits (for them), and by the desire to compete with other companies at home and abroad who are trying to do exactly the same. 'People?' says this system, 'What are they?'

Technology and progress

There was a time before this technological take-over when people developed a wide range of skills which allowed them to do most things for themselves. But the wrong kind of technology has de-skilled our society and made us more dependent. The move towards people specialising in one skill or one subject means we have to do jobs we often don't like to pay people to do jobs for us that we don't have the time or the skills to do for ourselves. Many of the abilities we acquire in specialised jobs are useless to us outside that particular workplace. We are learning more and more about less and less. One urgent priority of a Green government would be to provide the means to re-skill our society and remove this reliance on a full-time job.

If we phase out our total dependency on the world market by limiting imports and exports, we have the freedom to use the tax system to encourage the use of human creativity in the workplace and discourage the use of inappropriate technology. Today it happens the other way round. Technology should only be used if it serves people in the widest sense, not if people serve it.

This is a crucial point. If our values are shaped to a large extent by the system, what shapes the system? Technology. It is technology that took people off the land into the mills and the mass production factories. It is technology that has ravaged the countryside by creating the new farming methods. Technology has dictated how people live, where they live, where they work, whether they work, what they produce, how they produce it, and almost everything we do and buy. It has pulled us along with its every whim because we have always had the idea that if something has been invented it must be used. How often have we heard it? 'You can't stop progress.' Nor should you, but what we have done is confuse real progress in human and environmental terms with mere scientific advancement. The two are nothing like the same thing. Just because you can do something new doesn't make it necessarily good. Was the incredible technological achievement of inventing the atom bomb really progress?

We must tame this technological monster and not just sit there passively allowing it to control us. Green technology enables people to do things for themselves in their own communities at the lowest cost to their own pockets, their own creativity and inventiveness, and the planet's life support processes. It means a far greater emphasis on the small than the large, on tools rather than automation, on community businesses on a human scale rather than what Schumacher called 'giantism'.

We are told by the system that it's 'uneconomic' to go down this road. Only massive high-energy, low-people machines can pay, they say. We should not be surprised at this. Those with vested interests have predicted economic disaster with every attempt to increase human dignity, be it the abolition of slavery or the ban on children going up chimneys or down the mines. Those organisations that are producing human-scale technology appropriate to specific needs have shown these 'uneconomic' claims to be nonsense. They have shown that it is possible to make products locally for local consumption by developing low-energy, low cost technology that complements human skills rather than replacing them. It also allows more people to start up in business without facing the colossal costs of buying giant machinery which, at present, keeps most people out of the game and allows money (those with the capital) to go to money (so they have even more capital). This is how the rich get richer and effectively control the lives of the rest.

If you produce farming machinery for the Third World, for instance, which is costly to buy, run, and maintain, then you force all but the rich off the land. If you produce a plough that is highly efficient at turning over the soil when pulled by an ox then you open up opportunities to everyone, irrespective of means, and you help them to be less dependent. That is a simple example, but the same principle can be applied to the higher technologies turning out products that we need. We don't have to have all our giant factories that de-humanise work and concentrate power. The technology exists or can be developed that can share out the production to local communities producing for the community by using human skills on a human scale. The emphasis then would be on quality and not just quantity.

This doesn't mean that small is beautiful literally whatever you are producing. The word is *appropriate*. Every community would not have its own car manufacturer or fridge manufacturer, but so much can be produced by local people for local people in a truly efficient way if more have a say in the direction technology should go. Green technology enables, grey technology disables.

We now find ourselves in a spiral in which technology is replacing people, so the system has to keep expanding to provide jobs for those displaced by technology. As the race goes to lower costs and raise profits, those jobs are themselves replaced by machines and we have to expand again. Once more you can see the built-in self-destruction. By the time we have expanded enough to eliminate unemployment, the Earth will be a wasteland.

The limits to growth

The environmental limitations of expansion are now becoming obvious and the cost of natural resources on which technology and expansion depends is going to rise sharply as they become harder to extract. You'll notice how we are being forced into more inaccessible and inhospitable parts of the world in the search for oil and other resources. The easy sources are being sucked dry by the insatiable system and prices are bound to soar with serious consequences. Just because you hear about an oil glut on the world market from time to time doesn't mean there is a glut of it in the ground. It means the producers are so desperate to profit from it that there is more on sale at certain times than even our system can consume.

Oil is a good example of the way we are dependent on the unpredictable and the finite. Oil is not just energy from a power station. It is the fuel for most of our transport. It is chemicals. It is fertiliser and plastics. It props up the system. We are oil addicts every bit as much as heroin addicts are dependent on their drug. If we don't see that and make sensible decisions that wean us off our oil dependency, the outcome will be too horrific to contemplate.

Green economics

It doesn't have to be like this. What's more, it can't be. The Green Party would therefore take us in a quite different direction.

We would turn the economy on its head and make it cheaper to do the right thing than the wrong thing. At the moment the system makes it cheaper to throw things away and go back to the Earth for more than to re-use what we've already taken. This is thoroughly irresponsible and inefficient. A Green economy would be highly efficient in the true sense – and thrifty. Yes, that's the word; thrifty.

We would tax goods according to how long the products were made to last. The longer they were designed to last, the smaller the tax, while those things currently made to throw away would be taxed heavily, unless they were essential for medical purposes. So if, for instance, you make razors to last a life-time, the blades apart, then the tax system would support you. If you make plastic disposable razors, you would see their price rise considerably. People would not have to buy the same thing again and again. Throughput would be reduced along with pollution and the use of natural resources.

Another part of this throughput reduction is our policy of ensuring that products have to be made so they can be repaired and that spare parts are available throughout their projected life-time. Most of us have taken something back to the shop only to be told it would be cheaper to buy a new one than have it repaired. This is a terrible way to treat future generations. Companies make things this way because the throughput system could not survive if they didn't. Green politics would change that mentality and while work would be lost in the throwaway industries, it would be created in the far more people-based and personally satisfying repair business that will emerge rapidly. One report showed that if you make cars to last as long as possible, you lose half the jobs in motor manufacturing which are soul-destroying anyway, but you gain 50 per cent more jobs overall because of the repair and reconditioning businesses that would be needed to keep the cars running over a much longer period than they do today.

Billions of pounds are spent in research to fuel the throughput system and make us dissatisfied with what we have. Televisions, radios, and video recorders have been perfectly adequate for some time, but still the scientists and researchers waste minds and money to produce 'the latest thing' when both are urgently needed elsewhere. It is the same in almost every industry.

The Green Party would increase the cost of natural resources to make it cheaper to re-cycle resources already used than to dump them and go back to the Earth for more. The tax would be phased in alongside a massive expansion in recycling. Every day local authorities dump 30 million tons of solid waste; half of it comes from our dustbins. Every year the average family throws away six trees worth of paper and 624 plastic bottles, plus a fantastic amount of other 'rubbish'. Most of it can be recycled to spare the Earth further punishment, but the system doesn't want to know. We do. Natural resource taxes would also increase the price of goods with a high resource content and discourage their purchase. Our policies would also put an end to excessive packaging. All these measures would slow down the system of take, make and throwaway that threatens to destroy us. Although work would be lost in waste disposal and resource extraction, jobs would emerge in the recycling industries.

There would be fewer jobs in road building and road haulage as we moved from centralised to community economies, but smaller scale local businesses always mean more work than automated central production. Our policies on agriculture and energy would also create more work than they offer today.

The difference is that the Green way provides long-term, creative work by protecting the Earth while the throughput system provides precarious jobs (though not for everyone) by destroying it.

What kind of work?

But let's not delude ourselves. There won't be full-time jobs for everyone. There can't be and, frankly, nor should there be. Do we really believe that we were put on this Earth to have children and families and friends and then spend most of our time away from them? Were we really put here for millions of us to spend most of our waking hours looking at the clock praying for the hands to move a bit quicker because we hate what we do? Were we really put here to spend 40 hours a week, sometimes more, turning out fizzy drinks that damage children, chemicals that damage the ozone layer, useless plastic nick-nacks or whatever some smart marketing man can persuade the public it is trendy to possess?

Is that really what we are here for? Is it really? Or is it just possible that we are here to express the vastness of human potential in all its magnificent forms? Surely that is a more worthy celebration of life.

Today our true potential is being stifled and strangled by the throughput system. Most people don't have the time or the opportunity to realise our real talents because we are too busy working to survive or earning money to spend on the purely material things the system conditions us to want. Work is important to us and we should not underestimate how much good work lifts the human spirit. Much of our potential can be expressed in work if it is socially useful and demands skill, inspiration and creativity. But how much of our potential can we develop if we spend our lives as a mere cog in a production process or behind the wheel of an articulated lorry?

We must see the difference between work that develops human talents and does not threaten the planet and that which is merely a job we are forced to do by the system to serve the system.

Walter Schwarz put it like this: 'I need a job to earn the money to consume sufficient goods to keep other people in jobs. Since everybody wants to be better off next year, the system requires incessant growth to sustain it even though growth, like the cancer it is, will destroy the planet'. That's the treadmill we are on and it is turning faster.

Thankfully, there is another way. We would change the approach to work so that people are involved in making the whole product whenever possible and they would not just be a screw-turner on a production line. This is much easier to achieve when economic activity is moved from the centre to the community and you make quality products to last using human-scale technology with the emphasis on tools and not automation. Where unsatisfying, mind-numbing work needs doing, these are the areas that should be handed over to automation.

The Labour Party and socialism doesn't think of work in this way. They are still addicted to the concept of full-time 'jobs' for everyone instead of looking critically at the kind of work people are being forced to do. They also confuse jobs with work. A job is something formal that you get a set wage for. Work is much wider than that and includes all we do in the home and in the community. Much of this work is very satisfying and rewarding and socially necessary – anything from running the local youth club to caring for disabled relatives to running a charity. Without all this work that goes on outside a formal 'job' the economy could not operate. We should not think that because people don't have a full-time 'job' they don't work. Tell that to anyone who runs a home and looks after a family!

We want to free people to mix formal and informal work through part-time jobs and job sharing, and to give them access to those most precious of commodities, time and choice. To do that you need to underpin the reduced wage from the 'job' by giving everyone a share in the nation's wealth, which is another key reason for the Basic Income Scheme. Disposable time will also enable people to do more work for themselves which at present they pay someone else to do. This will in turn mean they need less disposable income. Others will prefer to continue in full-time formal employment and that's all right, too. It's their choice. Green economics has the flexibility to give them that choice.

Breaking the spell of the work ethic

Unfortunately, our society has come under the spell of the work ethic which people take to mean a full-time job. Somehow you are lazy or letting the side down if you don't spend the greater part of your life in this way. This highly destructive phenomenon was developed as a tool for the few to master the majority. This is why the ancient leaders told people the gods would be angry if they didn't work hard. The leaders couldn't lose. If there was a storm or natural disaster, the people were told the gods were angry and they must work harder. If there wasn't a storm or natural disaster, the people were told the gods were pleased they were working so hard and they should keep it up!

From such beginnings did the work ethic enslave us.

Dependency has brought this about. When we were hunters in the forests we were dependent on noone but ourselves and those who hunted with us. Now we are dependent on so many things controlled by so few that we cannot live our lives as we would wish. The few call the shots. The Green Party's economic policies are designed to restore as much of that control as possible. Dependency controls what we do; a lack of dependency gives us the control.

If you ask me if the richest few will have as much money as they have today (though not for too much longer as the source of wealth is destroyed) then the answer is no. Will anyone be earning a million pounds a year? No, I doubt it. But need anyone be hungry or forced to live in the street through lack of money? Certainly not. And wouldn't you feel good about living in a society that didn't turn out human debris as one of its waste products?

The Green Party would replace the growth obsession with what we call a Steady State Economy. I stress that contrary to popular myth, this would *not* mean no growth at all. When Greens talk of no growth, we mean no growth – and indeed an annual decline – in the rate of use of natural resources. This is the key to pulling back the reins on environmental destruction.

Reducing natural resources consumption has many effects; it slows down the process of turning irreplaceable resources at one end into pollution at the other; it means that they cease to be wasted; and it leaves more natural wealth for future generations.

It also means that a Green economy would have to be highly efficient because it would be getting more from less; waste would be reduced to an absolute minimum. Consequently there would be enormous growth in many areas like re-cycling, repair businesses and energy conservation, but these would be offset by phasing out the throwaway industries and those that rely on irreparable or very costly environmental damage.

This doesn't mean the economy would stagnate. There would be plenty of scope left for the entrepreneur, much more than now for small businesses and for those with little capital, and we are not talking about a society in which everyone is paid the same, irrespective of effort or contribution. The Green economy would ensure that no one was in poverty (through the Basic Income) while also guaranteeing that we did not destroy the base on which all wealth depends (nature's tolerance level).

The classic steady-state system is the Earth itself. Things are constantly evolving, growing, declining, emerging and dying, but the whole never gets any bigger. How appropriate, then, that our economics would work on exactly the same principle.

All this would obviously take time to phase in and our first priority would be to stop things getting worse before beginning the process of restoration. When you want to get out of a hole you first have to stop digging and that means being thrifty and responsible at the personal, local, regional, national and international level. The problem with the grey politicians is that they think the way to get out of a hole is to dig even faster. We would replace today's play-school economics, the Westminster

Fantasy, with simple commonsense that puts people and the planet first.

Do that, and the dragon, fierce as it is, would slowly but surely come to heel.

4: People power

*It will ever remain incomprehensible that our generation,
so great in its achievements of discovery, could be so low
spiritually as to give up thinking.*
ALBERT SCHWEITZER

It is far too late for tinkering with the environment, far too late
for putting the sticking plaster below the waterline when what
we really need are the life-boats. When the Titanic is sinking,
you don't just re-arrange the deckchairs.

If the structure of the economic system is the problem then
you have to change that structure and allow people to control
it. At present it controls the people. To stop this, political and
economic power has to be taken from the few at the centre and
handed to people in their own local communities.

The system of politics and business today is destructive, anti-
democratic, highly inefficient and takes power from the majority
and gives it to the few. In this way, the control we have over
our own lives and environments is constantly eroded. Until this
power is given to people in their own communities, they will
never have the chance to decide their own destiny. Someone at
the centre will do it for them.

First, there is no credible argument left against proportional
representation. The opposition to it comes from those politicians
who know that if we had real democracy in this country they
would no longer win total power with the support of just 32
per cent of the electorate. We don't have democratic elections
in this country, we have a sham, a sleight of hand. We can't
solve our environmental problems, or any others come to that,
until we have a parliament that represents the values and beliefs

of all the population. But that, in itself, is not nearly enough. If we just elect those people to govern our lives from far away, then apart from being more representative, power would stay with the few at the centre.

Handing back the power

The Green Party would devolve power in a very big way. Every decision that could be made locally would be made locally, every decision after that which could be made regionally would be made by new regional governments, and only those decisions that needed a national response or policy would be made in Westminster. It is a natural human reaction to want to control our own lives. The desire for regional and local autonomy is getting stronger all over the world, especially in the Soviet Union where rule from the centre has been so destructive and unjust.

Local councils would become the key decision-makers with the regions having the power to stop the decisions of one council harming another, and national government in the same way could step in if the decisions of one region were harming another. To emphasise where the power lies, taxes would be collected locally and a proportion handed over to the regions and Westminster. We would transform the approach to government so it was built from the bottom, not dictated from the top. The Green Party doesn't want power in the sense of taking it all for itself. The first thing we would do in government is start the process of handing as much power as possible to the communities where it should really be held. Once local people were making decisions for themselves, a tremendous amount of destruction would stop immediately. There would have to be proper discussion and consultation about development in all its forms and referenda would be encouraged on the big issues.

At present governments and councils are elected by a minority of the vote; then off they go to do what they like until the next election. We want ongoing public participation so that fundamental changes to communities cannot take place if the people don't want them. In this way we would have conservation and environmental protection built into the system because communities are not going to allow their areas to be scarred or poisoned if they have more power to stop it. They have to live there, after all. Every local community would become in effect its own environmental protection agency able to determine what is acceptable and what isn't on environmental grounds. Any disputes would be settled at regional level, not in Westminster.

Today decisions are taken by people who do not have to live with the consequences of what they decide. This is why so many bad decisions are made. Why are appalling planning decisions made by central government nearly always opposed by the local MP even if they are a member of the same party? Because they have to live with the consequences, the minister doesn't.

Is it any wonder that there is so much apathy about when people have been removed from the real decision-making process for so long? That apathy can only be removed if people believe that this involvement can have an effect on the outcome. We would encourage and support the setting up of community and neighbourhood councils so that everyone had the chance to contribute.

People tend to think that because many of the problems are global, the answer must be global. It is true that we must constantly seek international agreements and ways of enforcing them, but there are so many environmental problems that the main answer lies not in one all-encompassing solution which will never appear, but in all of us taking responsibility for ourselves and our communities. Yes, there must be transnational co-ordination; but only by all of us acting locally, and having the power to do so, can the planet be healed.

The cost of big business

As with government, so with industry and business. Power and control have moved away from people and been seized by the centre. With every take-over the control over our lives is handed to fewer and fewer people. At present a company wanting to take over another has to show that it is not against the public interest. We would make them show it is *in* the public interest – and on that basis the number of takeovers would virtually dry up. This is because most takeovers are not in the public interest, but in the interests of shareholders and boards of directors or in the name of increased prestige and status. Frankly, those reasons are not good enough.

These major companies and multi-nationals wield enormous power and control over countries as well as communities. That's not surprising when you see that the turnover and profits of these companies and corporations are greater than the incomes of many Third World countries. As a result the economies of those countries are run on behalf of the multinationals and not the people, something I will be looking at in more detail later.

We would discourage these power blocs in this country with a tax based on company size. The bigger the company, the bigger the tax, and this would help smaller firms to compete because they wouldn't pay it. It is not a case of small is best whatever the circumstances, but we do want to see a change to more smaller companies and an end to the present trend of a few giants swallowing up the rest and controlling local markets from afar. We do, however, most certainly need international agreement if we are really to curb the abuses of multinational companies.

We would use the tax system again to encourage what big organisations there were to devolve their power from the centre to semi-autonomous companies in which employees could take part in decision making. These large, faceless organisations which control everything by central dictat are often unpleasant to work for and very inefficient because they do not use their greatest asset: the knowledge, experience, and talents of their own workforce. It's all too impersonal and distant for these assets to flourish.

Schumacher likened the ideal business structure to a series of balloons all freely floating by themselves with a hand at the centre lightly holding the strings to keep them all together. You can apply this to all large businesses and to central government. It is the opposite of rule from above which Green Politics so opposes.

The more you centralise production, the more massive lorries you need to deliver that production and the further people have to travel to work. The results of that in pollution and wasted natural resources every year is shameful. The number and size of the lorries and the distances they travel, the number of commuters and the distances they travel have soared because of this centralisation.

If much more of the production and distribution were based locally there would be no need for all this waste because there would be no long distances for vehicles or people to travel every day. We would actually be able to spend more time with our husbands, wives, children and friends, something the present system is denying us more and more. The new communications technology makes this much easier to do.

On the Isle of Wight, we see the ferries unload enormous lorries every hour through the day – and off they go to create traffic problems, choke pedestrians with their cancer-causing fumes, damage roads that were not designed to take them or force the council to widen and repair roads with the community's money. These are just a few of the hidden costs of our 'efficient' centralised production.

What makes it all so ridiculous is that the Isle of Wight could produce most of the things these lorries bring in small scale businesses that would create local employment, end the need for bigger roads and constant repairs, and make it a much more pleasant environment in which to live. Instead of being dependent on one or two industries as most places are, local production for local need would spread the variety of employment, so if an industry closed down or declined it would not destroy the entire local economy. Again it reduces dependency and increases security and control.

There are endless costs that are never added to the debit sheet when companies talk about 'rationalisation' or whatever the latest buzz word may be. We and the environment pick up the tab for these costs, not the companies. They make it all sound so sensible. 'If we concentrate our production on one site we save this cost or that cost. We can increase our profit margins and produce more output.'

Jolly good. Most impressive. But what do this growth and these increased profit margins mean for us as a country and community? They mean more giant lorries to deliver goods longer and longer distances, and more cars to deliver people longer and longer distances.

We see our taxes that could go to much better use being spent on new roads and motorways, the price of which has long since entered cuckoo land and the environmental impact of which is horrendous; we see our city communities torn apart by urban motorways to 'speed' the transit of lorries and commuters to and from their centralised production and administration; we see thousands killed every year in road accidents and many thousands more injured with all the costs to them, their families, and the National Health Service; we see buildings damaged, roads damaged, sewers and water mains damaged; we see our trees dying from acid rain caused by exhaust emissions; we see all the stress and misery caused by living alongside roads full of heavy lorries. We see more ill-health. The list goes on and on. We and the planet cannot afford to be this 'efficient'.

You can appreciate what these costs add up to when you consider that one 38 ton lorry does more damage to a road than at least 100,000 cars. Next time you pass yet more road works remember that you are looking at one of the costs of moving production away from communities and to the centre. These are the costs the grey parties never talk about when they allow this system to go on.

What is so sad is that they are going in precisely the wrong direction. The Open European Market (known as '1992') will accelerate this process of moving production further away from people and into Europe. This will mean even bigger lorries travelling even longer distances, causing even more damage. For this reason and many others, 1992 is not the golden opportunity the politicians crow about. It will be a human, economic and environmental disaster, the last throw of the dice for a dying, discredited system. For the same reasons, the Channel Tunnel is one of the most gigantic wastes of money and resources it is possible to perceive.

The Green Party is so different in its approach. It looks behind the accountant-speak and the biased, misleading balance sheets to make the connections between events and find the real costs of any course of action. The pollution costs alone of this centralisation around the world are as colossal as they are obvious. Once again local production for local need has built-in environmental protection.

On the Isle of Wight we have a situation typical of the present system. The crops grown here go across the water to market on the mainland while mainland crops of the same kind come over on lorries to the Island. It becomes even more farcical when local shops and restaurants are forced to buy Island-grown food at the mainland market and bring it back across the water!

In a Green economy, the price of goods would reflect the whole cost of their production and distribution. When we go into a supermarket and look at the prices on the shelves, we only see part of the cost we are actually paying for these products. The rest we pay in our taxes for all the hidden costs which are met by the community, not the supermarkets. We are, in effect, subsidising the profits of these companies. If their goods had to reflect all these costs in the price, businesses producing locally for local consumption would be able to compete by producing more cheaply than the centralised giants.

This approach would ensure that the cheapest food and goods would be the least damaging – the opposite of what happens today.

Building the local economy

What the Island and every other community needs are local co-operatives or companies which take the food from the farms and growers and distribute it to the shops. Only what is not needed for local consumption should go off for sale elsewhere. This allows local people much more control over food production. At the moment they have very little. The power lies with a handful of supermarket chains and big companies which call the tune throughout the food production industry. Only every now and again when the truth about a process is made public does consumer power force changes and often very limited ones at that.

Rank-Hovis-McDougal, Associated British Foods, and Spillers French hold 75 per cent of the market for bread and flour. Unilever sell 70 per cent of the margarine and Nestlé 20 per cent. Tate and Lyle control 60 per cent of sugar sales – and so it goes on. You may buy different brands, just as you may see different names above the shops, but in truth most are owned by the same few companies. Is that in our best interests?

One farmer who supplies a major supermarket chain told me he was forced to spray his produce with more poisons than he wanted because they insisted that every vegetable and fruit was roughly the same size and shape. This is food production for the eye, not the stomach. Yet these are the same companies who have the nerve to call themselves 'green' because they stock a few organic vegetables and have unleaded petrol on the forecourt. While the system allows, nay encourages, a few major chains to dominate and centralise food production we will never have control over what we eat.

Another disadvantage of centrally-based business is that when you spend your money at a supermarket or national chain-store most of that money goes straight out of your local economy and back to the centre. When you spend it at a locally-owned shop, most of it will re-circulate in your local economy because the shop or business owner lives there. This would happen even more if, under Green Party policy, as many suppliers as possible were based locally as well.

So when big supermarkets move into communities claiming to bring 'jobs' they are often doing nothing of the kind. They are sucking capital out of local communities. But the grey parties on the Isle of Wight are obsessed with attracting big national names when all that does is squeeze out local small business and send shop rents soaring. It is crazy thinking.

Instead we would support local business by introducing community banks which would have the task of investing local money in the local economy. The major banks are another way that capital is lost by communities. We invest our money in the major banks, but very little of that is invested locally. It might go to support destructive schemes overseas or into chemical companies and such like. We don't really know what they are doing with our money. With community banks we would. It would be invested all around us.

Community economies have the flexibility to respond to local needs and fluctuations. They can overcome some problems without money. The present system sees one answer to everything. If money is short because the economy is in a mess, it has no idea how to respond without causing hardship to large numbers of people. Green economics is not imprisoned by such narrow thinking.

When you have high unemployment (which is all the time these days) you have people with skills who cannot use them because no one will give them money in exchange for their labour. This means that they can't spend at the local shops and so these suffer, too. Without a job those skills are, in effect, locked inside them. This talent can be released even at a time of severe recession if those in government, local and national, can see beyond the limitations of money.

What is money? It is nothing more than a means of valuing work, goods and services and of exchanging that work for those goods and services. So why does it have to be the *only* means of exchange?

One alternative is LETS, the Local Employment and Trade System, which started in Canada and is now springing up in communities in many parts of the world. It works like this. A group of people get together and agree to start a LETS Group. Each person makes a list of the things they can do (anything from babysitting to accountancy to gardening) and a list of things they would like done for them. They then agree their own currency within the group. The Canadians call it green dollars, but you can call it what you like. These dollars don't physically exist, they are just a way of valuing goods and services.

Say group member A wants the front room painted, but does not have the money to pay for it. They will look down the list and find someone who has painting and decorating as one of their skills, call them member B. They agree a price, perhaps 50 green dollars. The price is easy because you make your invented currency the same value as real money. When the work is done, a phone call is made to the group co-ordinator with the message 'Credit member B with 50 green dollars and debit me, member A, with the same amount.' Member A now owes the group 50 green dollars worth of skills while member B has earned that same amount in whatever skills he or she may need from other members of the group. You may have come across some babysitting circles that operate on the same principle.

It is a simple way to exchange skills without actual money changing hands. In some places shops and businesses sell their wares partly in these green dollars. It means that if you can't afford enough food for your family because you can't find a formal job, then you can use your skills to work within the LETS Group and get extra food in that way. When goods from outside the group are needed, the paint for that front room for instance, then that would be paid for in real cash and the labour in green dollars.

It takes a lot of determination and effort to get these groups going, but they have been very effective at overcoming the worst effects of recession and unemployment and a Green government or local authority would support and encourage them. It is not something, I stress, that would take over from the money economy, but it can get round some of its serious limitations.

Less reliance on trade

If we continued our total and ridiculous dependency on imports and exports these locally-based economies would be slaughtered. So as these more self-reliant communities and regions were phased in, so we would phase out a substantial amount of our trade on the world market.

All this sounds odd, doesn't it, when we have been brought up on 'export or die'? But then much of the conventional wisdom we learn through school and through life turns out to be daft when you see the truth. You can't read a paper without being told that this must happen or that must happen because we have to compete on the world market. My reaction is nearly always, 'Why?' Good word that, *why*? If you say it often enough it can reveal an awful lot of nonsense.

Try this one. Why do we export a product across the world to one country while at the same time bringing back across the world that country's version of the same product? Who gains apart from the transport company? I don't know, but I know who loses. Who always loses? The planet in terms of needless pollution and diminished finite resources. There are also millions of lost jobs world-wide as companies are 'slimmed down' to compete against other countries.

While we make ourselves so dependent on the world market we will never have control over our own economy and our own environment. If you depend totally on international trade and another country comes up with a cheaper way of making something, then you have a choice. You can use that process yourself or lose out. It might be a bad process, it might be bad for people and the planet, but you are under pressure to go down the same road just to compete. So much environmental and human damage is done in the name of competing with the rest of the world. This is one major reason why corners are cut and liberties taken with our children's future. This is why people are under enormous pressure to live today by destroying tomorrow. The fierce competition on the world market is the motor to constant technological change which controls and disrupts our lives. It is all irrelevant to the needs of people and makes it almost impossible for human-scale technology to be introduced. Again we are talking about scientific advancement and not about progress.

The system demands winners and losers, sets people against people, community against community, country against country in brutal competition. While the winners proclaim their economic greatness, the losers around the world die in their millions before their time. This is what 1992 is really about; winners and losers. If you open all the European Community countries to free competition, some have got to win and some, by definition, have got to lose in the bitter scramble for market domination. The terms in which we talk about trade reveal the truth. We talk of it almost as a kind of sporting contest. 'Britain is falling behind her European competitors . . . Germany is pulling ahead . . . France is coming through fast . . .'

Why should this have to be? Green international trade policy would be based more on co-operation than competition wherever possible. We want trade for mutual benefit, not winner takes all. For these reasons we would withdraw from the European Community unless there were swift and fundamental changes in the way it operates. We want to develop a Europe of regions which is not based on brutal competition and free-for-all trade.

There must, naturally, be a sector of the economy that competes internationally to pay for essential imports, but this sector would be a fraction of what it is today because our imports would be similarly curtailed. It will also provide comparatively little work because, for the reasons I've described, international competition will force this export sector down the road of more automation. Therefore the smaller this part of the economy has to be the better. The Green Party would limit other imports and exports by taxation to allow our policy of local production to grow and thrive. We would aim to limit trade as much as possible to mutual needs. Why should we be dependent on Japan and elsewhere for things we could make ourselves?

We would also have regard for the effect of our trade policies on poorer countries who would need special consideration in what we hope would be their transition to a similar economy. No one needs green economics more. Some of those countries are being ravaged by the injustices of the present trading system (see next chapter). But this reduction in trade is not a case of pulling up the drawbridge. The Green Party is the most international of parties and our communications and links with other countries must increase. Our trade policy is not aimed at isolation, but at efficiency and removing dependency.

This, then, is the basic structure of Green government and business. It takes power from the centre and gives it to people in their own communities; and by reducing so many of the present hidden costs, it is highly efficient in human and environmental terms. It promotes business and government on a human, personal scale so that everyone's talents and views can contribute. It does not import and export just for the sake of it, at the expense of people and the environment. It removes dependency on the powerful minority and gives control to the majority. The price of all goods, imports as well as home production, reflects the true cost of producing them.

All this could not be done overnight, obviously, though the work to introduce the new democracy would start immediately. Like many Green Party policies the aim is to implement them over a period. We have a period between now and the point within the life-times of today's young children when serious damage to the natural world is irreparable. Every day that passes is another day less to phase in these policies gently.

The longer we leave it, the quicker it will have to happen, because happen it must. For countless human and environmental reasons, the status quo is not an option.

5: Empty bellies and chocolate bars

The problem of the debt is political, more than financial, and should be confronted as such. What is at stake is not the accounts of the international creditors, but the lives of millions of people who cannot endure the permanent threat of the repressive measures and unemployment that bring poverty and death.

CARDINAL PAULO EVARISTO ARNS, METROPOLITAN ARCHBISHOP OF SAO PAULO, BRAZIL

It wouldn't be quite so bad if the system kept its nonsenses within its own borders, but it needs to expand and exploit elsewhere to survive.

That's how the economics and the way of life, in East and West, is causing such untold death, destruction and misery in poor countries throughout the world.

What would our reaction be if 160 fully laden jumbo jets crashed every *day* of every year with the loss of everyone on board? Words could not describe it, could they?

But that same number of people die every day from hunger and preventable disease for the 'crime' of being poor and exploited.

As Oxfam say in their book, *For Richer For Poorer*, we hear about the loud emergencies like the famine in Ethiopia which horrified us all. It filled our television screens for months and the public responded magnificently through Live Aid and other charities. But the full story is far worse.

Out of sight of the cameras every day, 800 million people, one in six of the human race, suffer from malnutrition.

As the second Brandt Report put it:

> Every two seconds of this year a child will die of hunger or
> disease. And no statistic can express what it is like to see even
> one child die ... to see the uncomprehending panic in eyes
> which are still the clear and lucid eyes of a child.

What makes it even more appalling, if that is possible, is that
many are dying so that the fortunate few in the rich world can
be richer still. They are dying so we can have 'freedom of
choice'.

Our responsibility

The system doesn't want you to have this kind of information
because it knows that once you have the facts it is in deep
trouble.

The aerosol makers knew for years that CFCs were destroying the ozone layer, but they did nothing. Profit came first. It
was only when the public had the information, thanks to Friends
of the Earth, that they stopped buying the aerosols and the
companies were forced to act.

So it is with hunger in the Third World.* The last thing the
system wants you to know is that it, and through it, *we*, are the
cause of most of the hunger. If the public in the rich world
knew the truth they might cause a fuss and that would not do.
They know we can use our buying power to force changes that
the system does not want to make.

There is this illusion, this tragic illusion, that we give money
to poor countries. It is even offered as proof that the system

---

* I dislike the term 'Third World', but I am using it because it is a term that
people easily understand. In this context I take the Third World to be countries
in which large numbers of people live in absolute poverty, though the incomes
and development of these countries may vary enormously, e.g. Brazil and
Bangladesh.

works. It's our old friend 'trickle down' again. If you allow some to get very rich then enough of their money will trickle down to the poor. I'm afraid it's not true.

The poorest countries on Earth give *us* more money than we give them. In 1988 43 billion dollars *more* went from poor to rich in a year than went the other way. The human and environmental consequences of that are catastrophic. We are bleeding them dry.

That $43 billion was in debt repayments alone. It doesn't begin to count the endless other ways we have of exploiting them. Goodness knows what the true figure might be.

Back in the 1970s when the Arab countries vastly increased the price of oil they invested their new wealth in Western banks and they, in turn, were desperate to re-invest it. They thought the best way to invest it safely was with Third World countries. Companies might fold and disappear, but countries would always be there to safeguard the investment.

So scores of young people, mostly in their twenties, were sent around the world offering enormous loans, often to despots and military governments who had no intention of spending that money to help the poor.

In fact on many occasions these corrupt politicians in concert with the banks actually re-invested large amounts of this money in their own names with the very same banks who had loaned the money in the first place. President Marcos in the Philippines was a classic example. He invested billions around the world by taking this loan money for himself – and there were many others. But still the banks carried on, because for them it was good business.

In their 1987 report Lloyds have a section called 'Serving Wealthy People Across the World'. It says: 'We [Lloyds International Private Banking Group] now have an international network to serve a growing number of international clients who have come to expect much the same treatment for their funds as a multi-national corporation. They demand not only a professional, personal and discreet service; they look for the ability to move funds across borders to best advantage.'

The money was loaned to these countries at variable interest rates. As those rates have gone up and the countries' incomes have failed to keep pace, so people have died in their millions or been condemned to constant hunger. Their environments have been devastated as they are forced to destroy tomorrow simply to survive another day.

In the dock are Western and Eastern governments, the commercial banks, multi-national companies, and the tiny rich élite they work with and support in the poor countries.

Cash crops and starvation

To pay back the loans, or for the profits of the Western multi-nationals and this rich élite, the poorest countries in the world grow cash crops on land that could be growing food for their own people. That's why Ethiopia was still exporting food at the height of the famine. That's why 400,000 children are reckoned to die in Brazil every year from hunger related diseases when Brazil is one of the biggest exporters of food in the world.

According to Oxfam, well over half the children in Ghana are malnourished while over half that country's foreign exchange is spent on repaying loans to the rich. This has meant cuts in health care, education, and even water supplies. And perhaps the most stunning fact of all: while all those children go hungry in Ghana, half, *half*, their farming land is not growing food for the malnourished, but COCOA FOR WESTERN CHOCOLATE BARS!

Our children eat chocolate bars while the bellies of children in Ghana stay empty. Hard to take, isn't it, and if you are ashamed of these facts I don't blame you. So am I.

But unless you go in search of the truth you will never find out these connections between our luxuries and their hunger. The system won't tell you, indeed it will do all it can to keep it from you.

It would not like you to know that 40 per cent of the food-growing land in Senegal is growing peanuts for Western margarine. It would be aghast if you found out that in Colombia where malnutrition is common, fertile land is used to grow cut flowers for the rich in the West. Or that even during the great drought in the Sahel, the production of peanuts for export increased there while tens of thousands starved.

In the name of decency, in the name of humanity, what is this system we are supposed to defend? A system that allows little children to starve when there could be food aplenty, allows people to go blind for the want of a few pounds, and to die from disease for the want of treatment costing a few pence.

Green politics is about personal responsibility and all of us must understand that when we buy products grown on the land of the hungry we are supporting the system that allows a child to die every two seconds. We are responsible, too, once we know the truth.

Every day throughout the forests of the poor world a time bomb ticks away as the environment is further degraded in the name of survival and massive profits for the few. Fertility is being destroyed by growing cash crops intensively on unsuitable land; logging concessions are sold to Western multi-nationals to cut down the rain forests; wealthy ranchers and multi-nationals cut down trees to graze cattle for our hamburgers; and the poor are forced to cut down more trees to grow food because all the agricultural land is growing for the rich.

Once the trees are gone the soil rapidly turns to desert and soon more trees come down. The burning of the forests pours carbon dioxide into the atmosphere, adding to the greenhouse effect. Living trees also act as 'sinks', taking carbon dioxide out of the atmosphere in their natural processes. With every tree lost another 'sink' is lost, adding yet more to global warming. Yet by the end of the century at the present rate of decline there will be little of our rainforests left.

If a Martian had spent the last 40 years observing the human race he would go back home and report no sign of intelligent life.

Forests also control the flow of water. They hold it back when there is too much – which helps prevent floods – and they release it gradually, which helps to lessen the impact of drought. So as trees have been burnt or cut down all over the Third World for survival or short-term profit, the number and severity of floods and droughts have grown enormously.

Trees are also crucial to retaining the soil. They help to bind it together, and to stop it being washed or blown away. As the trees disappear so does the top soil, the very basis of life. Yields fall, fertility is destroyed and eventually only sand is left behind.

Growth and the poverty spiral

Now what answer do you think the West is putting forward to tackle these problems? Yes, you've got it; more *economic growth*!

The idea is that the poor countries go for the export of cash crops to raise the money to (surprise, surprise!) buy in the goods they 'need' from the developed countries. This increasingly means importing food as well as the cars and luxury goods for the rich few. East and West get the raw materials they need at low prices so they can turn them into 'things' and sell them back at a profit to the Third World. This has made most poor countries dependent for their survival on one or two basic exports – and who sets the world price for those exports? We do.

Could these poor countries turn their own raw materials into 'things' and export them? Sorry, the rich countries impose trade barriers to prevent it. They are only interested in raw materials, thank you.

And if the world price for the commodity falls, or demand is reduced by a new production process? Tough.

When these countries get into desperate trouble and can't

repay their colossal debts to Western banks and governments, in comes the International Monetary Fund, the IMF. This is the system's police force, dominated by America and other rich countries like the UK, which makes sure everyone plays by the right rules. Theirs.

They go into a country and tell them they must cut public spending and increase exports, or else. The few rich people in the country must be allowed to get richer so there can be trickle-down, but subsidies on food for the poor must be cut and so must spending on health care and education. This has led to a new term in the Third World, the 'IMF riot'. These riots occur when people already hungry are told that food subsidies are being reduced. Would you not riot if you were told this when your children were malnourished?

The IMF also demands increased production of cash crops to raise more money and stimulate 'growth'. The problem is that so many countries are in this mess that if they all take this line there is a glut of their commodities on the world market. What happens? The price collapses.

So more land is taken out of food production for local need to grow more cash crops, but because the price drops they end up earning only the same or even less for their extra production than they did before. But who benefits from cheaper raw materials? We do.

No wonder a former employee of the IMF said there was not enough soap in the world to make him clean again after what he had done to the poor on behalf of the rich.

Britain's Overseas Development Ministry has also been at the forefront of linking our aid to 'Structural Adjustment Pro-grammes' like those adopted by the IMF.

The great frog massacre

The great frog massacre in India and Bangladesh gives you an idea of the kind of nonsense you get with the growth obsession.

The damp regions of these countries supported vast numbers of frogs. They were vital to local people because they fed off the pests that kill the crops and carry diseases like malaria. But unfortunately for the local people, France has exploited its own frog population to near extinction and the rest are protected by law, while Britain and other European countries are also getting a taste for frogs' legs.

The first disgusting fact is that the frogs are killed by pushing them down on to a vertical blade which cuts them in half. The top half, which can survive for up to an hour without its legs, is thrown away. The legs were sold for export. In 1978 alone, India exported the legs of nearly eleven thousand tons of frogs which would have eaten ten thousand tons of pests every day. This meant that they received £5.5 million for the frogs. But because the frogs were no longer eating the pests, the bill for imported pesticides to replace them was . . . £13 million!

The point is, though, that the rich elite sold the frogs' legs while the poor had to find the money for the pesticides, some of which are so dangerous they are even banned in the West. The poor suffer once again, but the transactions add to economic growth and that's all the people who run the system are interested in.

Finally, what did the European Community do when they heard of all this? Cry stop? Not quite. They paid for a group of frogs' legs exporters from Bangladesh to visit Europe to find new markets.

These arms of the system – like the IMF and the World Bank, also dominated by America – are responsible for the deaths of many millions of people and for the devastation of large areas of the planet. What these forces are doing to the native peoples of the forests and the poor countries in the quest for 'progress' and 'growth' is genocide, and nothing less.

The multi-nationals

The role of the multi-national corporations is particularly shocking. Many of them are household names to us and they are touchy about their image. If the truth got out it would not be good for business.

So you don't get told that in Kenya a subsidiary of Brooke Bond grows carnations for Western button holes while Kenya has some of the highest rates of malnutrition in the world.

Nestlé won't tell you that they dump free baby milk powder on hospitals in poor countries so the mothers are discouraged from breast-feeding. Once they leave hospital they are dependent on Nestlé baby milk and by then, of course, it is no longer free. Babies are dying because their mothers cannot afford the milk or because of the unhygienic conditions and dirty water in which it has to be prepared. Nestlé sells £24 worth of baby milk in the developing world every second. A baby dies from unsafe bottle feeding in the developing world every three minutes.

Volkswagen don't tell you they destroyed 181,470 hectares of Brazilian rainforest to produce the biggest cattle ranch yet created there. The fire was so big it showed up on a satellite picture.

It also slips the mind of BP in their quest to be 'green' that they have razed hundreds of thousands of acres of rainforest to increase their already colossal profits.

The power of the multi-nationals is fantastic. Even back in 1980, the 30 biggest companies and their subsidiaries had sales worth six times Britain's national income. Each of them has a turnover greater than 29 African countries put together. It is they who are in control of many countries, not the governments and certainly not the people.

The cause of this exploitation is the same as always. Power is in the hands of the few, who control the rest by making them dependent. That's what the system demands and that's what it gets. Many of these corporations buy up vast areas of food-growing land in the Third World, but they don't plant all of it. Some they just leave, because if the local poor do not have land to provide for themselves, they have got to work for the company for the wages and conditions the company decides. According to the book, *Food First*, 'The US giant corporation Del Monte owns 57,000 acres of Guatemala, but plants only 9,000 acres. This prevents peasants from using the land to grow food.'

The governments of these countries are either corrupt, desperate for foreign exchange, or egged on by the IMF and others. Whatever the reason they do whatever the multi-nationals want at the expense of the people. The small rich élites are also well looked after by the corporations, which ensures wild support from that quarter. This allows the multi-nationals to demand and be given agreements that their profits can be taken out of the country and back to head office. They even get periods when they pay no tax at all. When these periods are over some pack up and go somewhere else.

The multi-nationals have such a grip that around *half* of world trade involves trade between the subsidiaries of these companies! Naturally the profits made in poor countries don't stay there. It is just a paper figure. Every dollar invested by American companies in Latin America produces three dollars in profit that goes back to America.

The multi-nationals have other little tricks. When cigarette sales fall in the West in the face of medical evidence, you increase the promotion of smoking in poorer countries and get them hooked. When even the West bans a pesticide for being too dangerous, you sell it in the Third World, but you don't give them the safety equipment to use it. You tell them to put it on by piercing holes in a tin and shaking it. The World Health Organisation says that one person is poisoned by pesticides in the poor countries every minute. If your profits from chemical factories are reduced by the need to meet your own country's standards, low as they may be, you move your factory to a poor country and because of your power you run it how you like.

This book would have to match *War and Peace* to tell even a fraction of this story of callous disregard for human life and human dignity. What those corporations do is a scar on the face of humanity, but it makes the economic growth figure look wonderful. The trouble is you can't eat the economic growth figure.

The aid deception

Still, at least we give aid to poor countries don't we? Er, no. Actually, we give most of it to ourselves.

Let's put the aid into perspective first. War on Want estimate that British banks received around £3 billion in 1988 in debt interest payments alone from poor countries, yet Britain's aid budget for the entire world was less than half that, £1.3 billion.

What's more 71 per cent of our bilateral aid money goes directly to British companies.

America's aid is far less than it receives in profits from the poor, and 93 per cent of it is spent in America. In 1980, 4,000 American companies got $1.3 billion in this way.

Canada demands that at least 80 per cent of aid is spent on Canadian goods and services, and the story is the same throughout the rich world. Aid is not used to help the poor. It is a means of subsidising industry at home, and buying influence and control around the world for economic, military and political purposes. The Third World thought it had won its independence from Western control. It hasn't. Physical occupation has been replaced by financial occupation. This is vital for the system to survive. No exploitation. No system. Even aid is used to promote dependency.

Senator Hubert Humphrey of the United States gave the game away:

> 'I have heard,' he said, 'that people may become dependent on us for food. I know that was not supposed to be good news.

To me, that was good news, because before people can do anything they have to eat. And if you are looking for a way to get people to lean on you and to be dependent on you, in terms of their co-operation with you, it seems to me that food dependence would be terrific.'

Precisely. This is why aid does not go to the poorest on the basis of who needs it most. It is offered on the basis of what's best for the giver.

In 1986, Westland Helicopters put advertisements in the national press patting itself on the back for securing a deal with the Indian government to sell them 21 helicopters. Just as well because they needed the business. But hold on. It turns out the Indian government did not want the helicopters. They were paid for almost entirely by the British aid budget and India was told if they didn't accept this 'aid' they were unlikely to get it in any other form. Twenty-one helicopters paid for by aid when the receiver didn't want them; and yet the cost of just one of those helicopters represents the whole development programme for Ethiopia.

Then there is the Aid-Trade Provision so loved by British governments, Labour and Conservative. This means that if a British company is chasing a contract with a Third World country and the competition is getting tough they ask our government to help them. We offer the country a slice of the aid budget on the understanding that the British company gets the contract. Whether the country needs the aid or others need it more is irrelevant. As long as Britain wins the contract that's all that matters.

The West even dumps its food surpluses on the Third World in the name of aid. This puts local farmers out of business, so reducing still further the food produced for local need.

Every illustration I'm giving is not a rarity or a one-off. This is the way it works all the time. Yet despite all these facts, a Conservative Secretary of State for the Environment told his party conference that those who opposed today's economic system and the growth obsession should explain themselves to a poor peasant! It was one of the most offensive and astonishing remarks I had heard in many a year. It didn't seem to dawn on him that 100,000 people die from hunger-related disease every day under *his* system – not ours.

The arms trade

A great deal of aid has been given in arms, for goodness sake, which is just the thing to eliminate hunger isn't it? But if you want to exploit the poor through your aid budget and your banks, exploit them through multi-national companies, and by supporting despots and wealthy elites just because they do what you want, then you must expect that at some time the mass of the people are going to rebel against all this.

That's where the arms come in. That's where the propaganda comes in as well. You bring on the smokescreen called the Soviet Threat to justify your military support for the forced suppression of protest. The long overdue reforms in the Soviet Union under Mr. Gorbachev are making this old, tired line sound ever more hollow, but they still use it whenever people cry 'enough' and rebel after years of misery.

They use it to hide the truth and to prevent democratic governments taking power. The last thing the system wants is for the Third World countries to be run in the best interests of the local majority.

The CIA are always plotting to block or bring down any government they feel is not in the best interests of America. It doesn't matter how decent that government may be, if they won't have US military bases, or they want to stop exploitation by US multi-nationals, or they won't supply raw materials the US demands, then the skids will be put under them in every way possible.

Far fetched?

The US and its allies have armed the neo-fascist elites of the Third World to the teeth, and saturated them with counterinsurgency weaponry and training ... Hideous torture has become standard practice in US client fascist states ... Much of the electronic and other torture gear is US supplied, and great numbers of client state police and military interrogators are US trained ... The US is the prime sponsor of Third World fascism. (*The Washington Connection and Third World Fascism*, 1979.)

E. S. Herman in *The Real Terror Network* agrees:

Many of the world's brutal dictatorships ... are in place precisely because they serve US interests in a joint venture with local torturers at the expense of their majorities ... These policies of repression are ... designed to keep large numbers in a state of serious deprivation while small upper classes, multinational business interests and élites of military enforcers 'develop' these countries without any democratic constraint.

When people rebel against these horrors they are said to be doing it on behalf of the Soviet Union. It is not the Soviet Union or any other country that inspires rebellion; it is the evil injustices and brutality the people are forced to suffer by regimes propped up by America and others for financial, military and political ends.

The case of Nicaragua

Look at the story of Nicaragua. Oxfam produced a superb booklet which summed it all up in the title: *Nicaragua, The Threat of a Good Example?*

What terrifies the system more than anything else is the thought that a Third World country will control its own development, free itself from dependency, and that others will see its success and take the same course. That's why the United States, supported by Britain, has been determined to destroy Nicaragua.

The Somoza dictatorship controlled the country from 1936 until 1979. The presidency was handed down through the family. There were no democratic elections. They ruled by terror and murder. They took land from the poor and gave it to the rich. Members of the National Guard – terrorists, nothing more – made fortunes in this way, President Somoza more than anyone.

Despite this terrorism, Nicaragua attracted massive financial aid and support from the United States, Britain, and the system in general. It was given because Somoza played the game to suit them. Under him the country ran up debts of more than one and a half billion dollars, a shocking figure for a country of this size. When Somoza fled in 1979, the national reserves totalled just three and a half *million*.

At the end of Somoza's reign of terror, one baby in eight died before their first birthday; two out of three children were undernourished; six out of ten deaths were from preventable and curable diseases; less than 20 per cent of under fives and pregnant women received any health care; two out of three peasants had no land; 94 per cent of rural children could not even finish primary school; more than half the population was illiterate; 30 per cent of their tropical rainforests had been destroyed in ten years; and Nicaragua had the highest levels of deaths from pesticides in the world. The *Sydney Morning Herald* said it all:

> The Somoza family owned 30% of all land tilled in Nicaragua.
> Over the years, secured in power by unswerving loyalty from
> Washington, the Somoza family was able to turn Nicaragua
> into its personal fiefdom, growing enormously rich, while
> smothering all opposition in the name of fighting communism.

Same old story. Use the Soviet Threat to do what you please.

The cost to the people of overthrowing Somoza was staggering. 50,000 died. Homes, factories, schools and hospitals were destroyed by Somoza bombing raids. 45,000 children were made orphans. Add to that the debts left by Somoza that the country still had to pay back, and you can see what a task the new Sandinista Government faced in rebuilding the country.

They held democratic elections, which British MPs observed were fair, and set about the job along just the lines the Green Party has always promoted. Green politics is about enabling people to help themselves and that is what has happened in Nicaragua. Communities are given the materials and the tools and where necessary the expertise to build and develop their own communities in the way they see fit. People are given back control over their own lives and their own communities.

The transformation has been remarkable. By 1984 there were 127 per cent more schools, 61 per cent more teachers, and 55 per cent more children at primary school. More than 1,500 new schools were built, many by local people after the government provided the materials. In the first three years of the new government, illiteracy was halved. Under Somoza only 9,000 children enjoyed pre-school facilities and they were mostly the children of the rich. By 1984 70,000 under sixes attended mainly free day-care centres.

Under Somoza only a quarter of the population had access to regular health care. After three years of the new government it was 70 per cent. Vaccination rates were impressive even by British standards. According to the *New England Journal of Medicine*, 'In just three years, more has been done in most areas of social welfare than in fifty years of dictatorship under the Somoza family.'

In agriculture, the emphasis has moved from growing cash crops for rich landowners to growing food for the local people – and more land has been provided to do it.

Three weeks after the new government took over, a Nicaraguan Institute for Natural Resources was set up. It launched schemes for forest management, re-afforestation, water purification and pollution control. Alternative energy programmes have been started and the country aims to be self-sufficient in energy by the end of the century. 'Environmental consciousness' is now a key part of the education system.

The Sandinistas have built the Green way from the bottom up, not the top down. They have given people the power to do things for themselves. They have concentrated on providing for need and not greed. The World Council of Churches was most impressed:

> What we see is a government, faced with tremendous problems, some seemingly insuperable, bent on a great experiment which, though precarious and incomplete at many points, provides hope to the poor sectors of society, improves the conditions of education, literacy and health, and for the first time offers Nicaraguan people a modicum of justice for all, rather than a society offering privilege exclusively to the wealthy . . . and to the powerful.

But why is this great crusade still 'precarious and incomplete'? Because the United States, supported by Britain and other Western countries, is desperate to bring down the government and go back to business as usual. It started a trade embargo. Financial backing is now but a trickle. Our own government's record on this is a national disgrace. We gave far more aid to the evil Somoza in his last years in power than we do to the democracy that replaced him. What was worse, however, was that the United States funded a terrorist army, the Contras, dedicated to seizing power from the elected government. Under Reagan and Bush it tried to use money from arms sales to Iran to further fund the Contras against the wishes of Congress in the famous Colonel North debacle.

The terror that the people of Nicaragua thought was ended with the overthrow of Somoza was still with them – and it was paid for by the United States. This is what they got for their money:

'The Contra attacked us at 11 a.m. I was in the kitchen. They began with mortars. There were about 600 of them. We only had 20 militia. One of the mortars fell and killed an old woman in the shelter. When they got nearer, my little sister begged them: "You already killed an old woman, please don't kill our children."

But they tortured and slit the throats of our militia. I know, because there were so few and they had no more ammunition, they gave themselves up with their hands in the air. And when I got out, they had castrated one of the boys and cut another's tongue out. And a militia girl who was four months pregnant, they raped her and cut off her breasts while she was still alive. They left them all naked. Then they burned them.' (*The words of a villager of Castillo Norte, quoted by Oxfam.*)

To give you an idea of the scale of these attacks, 7,000 Nicaraguan civilians were killed by the Contra 'freedom fighters' in the two years to 1984 alone. Nearly half of them were children. Scores of teachers and doctors were murdered in the villages, countless schools and health centres were destroyed along with key sectors of the economy. Around 40 per cent of the country's income was committed to fighting the Contras, and the great social and welfare advances were threatened.

When you look at what has already been achieved for the poor since Somoza, just think what could be done if it were not for the United States' determination to run every country for its own benefit.

A green approach to aid

The story of Nicaragua shows perfectly why there is starvation and misery throughout the Third World and how quickly it can be eliminated if we develop in the way the Green Party has always promoted – community economies with local people in control. There is much more we would like the Nicaraguan government to do before it could be called truly green, but they have already proved beyond doubt that hunger and suffering are not facts of life. It doesn't have to be like this.

We would take a whole new approach to Third World aid and development. The Aid-Trade Provision would be abolished and aid would be offered only on the basis of who needs it most. It would cease to be used as a hidden subsidy for British industry and would be channelled instead into projects that directly help the poor. The people themselves would tell us what they needed. (Today we tell them. This is why they get massive dams and motorways which only help multi-national corporations and the rich.) The aid that really makes the difference between suffering and survival is that which provides basic agricultural equipment and seeds to grow food, improved health care and education, safe water supplies and new forests.

This approach would reduce the economic growth figure on which current development is based and expose it for the nonsense it is. Dams and motorways massively increase economic growth. Ploughs and health care do not. But they do stop children dying every two seconds.

We would not provide food aid except in an emergency and we would certainly not dump our surpluses and claim we were being generous. Security and freedom is growing food for yourself, not depending on some distant authority to sanction a lorry load of grain.

The Green Party would set up an Aid Advisory Council made up of government, the aid agencies, charities, churches, and other people with the right experience to decide the best way to use the aid budget. Aid would be given to Third World governments only if we were satisfied it would be used properly. We would assess a government on its record of democratic and human rights, land reform and the treatment of the people – not on whether they played the game to the West's advantage.

If there were any doubts the aid would go directly to the people via the aid charities.

Our entire policy is aimed at making the poor self-sufficient in staple foods and other basic needs and freeing them from dependency and exploitation. We would seek to ensure, through encouragement and financial support, that land was used to grow food for all the local people as the first priority; and that only land left over after those needs were satisfied was turned over to cash crops for export. We must end the inhumanity that allows people to starve while their land is used to grow money for multi-nationals and rich landowners.

Ending the debt crisis

To do this, the debt crisis must be resolved. People are dying under the burden of debt that is not of their making. While the debt is there they will always have to use large areas of land for cash crops to keep up the payments. We would write off the debts of the poorest and limit repayments from the others to ten per cent of annual earnings. We would also establish a scheme that would both remove debt and replenish and repair the environment. It is called Creative Re-imbursement, or debt-for-nature swops.

Local development funds would be set up in all Third World countries that agreed to take part and all the money their governments paid to their fund would be matched by a reduction in foreign debt. The funds would be run by local people and they would spend the money on environmental restoration, planting forests, protecting the soil from erosion, and generally creating the conditions in which nature can heal herself. They would also establish small-scale community economies run by local people for local people.

Obviously we could only do this at first with the money owed to Britain, but we would do all we could to persuade the other rich countries to do the same. These measures would apply to both the government and commercial banks.

'Oh, but look what this will cost us!' some people cry. Well, three things about that. First, it is *not* a great deal of money when set against the wealth we have – and anyway, much of that wealth has come from exploiting these very countries. Second, the devastation of Third World environments like the rainforests threatens all of us. Third, we don't, frankly, have a choice. The world financial system is holding on by its finger tips. It has so over-reached itself with loans which Third World countries cannot afford to repay that it is now being forced to lend them more money to keep up the payments on the previous loans! They are putting off for just a little while longer the day when we could face a financial collapse on a global scale. Unless strong, responsible governmental action is taken now the debt crisis could engulf us all.

Restraining the multi-nationals

So to the multi-nationals. If there is to be justice and environmental protection, their power must be diminished and preferably disappear in the longer term.

A Green Party government would monitor the operations of the multi-nationals all over the Third World through local representatives and the United Nations Centre on Trans-National Corporations (which we want to see expanded and strengthened.) Regular reports would be issued to the widest possible audience on their abuses of power and names would be named. Public relations agencies would no longer be able to promote a fake respectability for these corporations while in truth they were causing misery and hunger for millions. The public would be told and that is bound to show itself in lost profits.

We would further make it illegal for any company to export any products, including chemicals and pesticides, that were banned in Britain. We would also press for laws within the European Community to set out regulations for multi-nationals to observe all over the world. These would relate to their treatment of people and the environment. Any corporation which ignored these regulations would be prevented from operating in Europe.

A Green government would do all it could to break up these all-powerful giants into smaller, less powerful units on at least a national and ideally a regional basis.

They stand accused of a criminal abuse of power and the time has come to take vigorous action before that power becomes absolute.

I have only sketched the foundations of Green Party policy in this area, but I hope I have made it clear why injustice and environmental destruction are linked at every turn. It is the rich world's exploitation of the poor that is behind the ecological disaster, and it should shame us all. We said we would never let the holocaust happen again. We have. It is being done in our name today.

We are supporting it, unknowingly, at the supermarket check-out.

6: Baby boom

For the first time I am running scared for the future, for though I know we can solve the problems of poverty, starvation and environmental misuse, there is no future unless the population bomb is defused now.
DAVID BELLAMY

The global figures are stunning.

It took from the birth of humankind until 1830 for the population of the world to reach one billion. The second billion took 100 years. The third billion took 37 years. The fourth billion took 13 years. It is now over five billion and will be six billion by the end of the century.

In the time it takes your heart to beat once, two babies are born. The population of China alone now exceeds the population of the entire planet 200 years ago. Indeed, if the population growth of recent times had begun with the birth of Christ, there would now be 900 people for every square yard of ground. The Earth and all forms of life upon it cannot survive this scale of human intrusion.

There are, however, some myths about population that we must dispel. Despite what many believe, starvation is not caused overall by the size of the population. Poverty, and exploitation by the rich, cause that. The Earth can still provide for everyone if everyone is given a fair share.

There is another myth that says it is just a Third World problem. Yes, the population explosion in terms of numbers is happening in those countries, but their individual impact on the Earth is far less. A baby born in the rich world will grow up to consume 40 times more of the Earth's resources than will the babies of the poor. It is a problem for all of us and we must address it.

While exploitation is the cause of hunger, it does not take a genius to work out that a population cannot continue to soar while their home, the Earth, stays the same size. There may in theory be enough land to feed many more people than we have even today, but much of that land is being degraded and destroyed. As the population grows so more space is needed and more wildlife disappears as their habitat is taken or they are killed for money or food.

Water supplies cannot cope with these increases in population when they are already being sucked dry by intensive farming and industrialisation in the poor countries. The rising sea levels caused by global warming also threaten to pollute ground water.

You cannot eat or drink theory and it is no good people sitting back and saying the population explosion would not be a problem if we lived in a different world. Our actions today must be based on how things are, not on how we would like them to be. The truth and reality is that exploitation and massive population increases are leading us along the road to catastrophe. Both for the billions who will suffer directly and the rest in the rich countries who will also face the consequences of the environmental slaughter that will ensue.

Why, then, do the grey parties never mention population in their manifestos? Because once again they think it will not go down well with the electorate; rather than be responsible, they ignore it. The Green Party does not ignore it. You can't when you see what is happening.

In 1987, Africa had a population of 480 million. Within 40 years it is projected to be around 1,544 million. Ethiopia will increase from 46 million to 65 million by the turn of the century, while losing a billion tons of top soil every year through erosion caused by deforestation and inappropriate farming methods. Nigeria's population is now 100 million, but sixty years from now it is projected to be 532 million! And in Bangladesh, the most densely populated country in the world, numbers are likely to rise from 101 million to 145 million by the year 2000. This in a country the size of England.

The scale of the suffering that is about to unfold unless things change is beyond my comprehension.

There are many reasons for this explosion in human numbers, one of the main ones being the falling death rates around the world this century. None of the answers are simple or easy and if the Green Party is involved none of them will ever include compulsion or coercion. We find that idea totally repugnant.

The answers lie in four main areas: the elimination of poverty, the emancipation of women, availability of birth control, and education.

The elimination of poverty

When you are a parent in a country with no pensions or social security, you depend on your family for survival in old age. You have a lot of children because you see this as adding to your security, especially when you know that some will almost certainly not make it through childhood because of hunger and disease. It's OK some people saying they should not have big families, but put yourself in their position.

I have also heard the view that the insecurity bred by the imposition of an alien culture is fundamental to the population problem. I have enormous sympathy with this. Edward Goldsmith, writing in *The Ecologist*, says that when a traditional society is replaced by 'growth' development, the population always explodes. He points out that the population of Britain was only eight million before the start of the industrial revolution, but it immediately took off to reach 57 million 200 years later. The same story is being repeated, he believes, throughout the Third World today.

It is certainly true that the population of traditional societies held steady for centuries. People lived in small groups who cared for each other. There was stability and security. You didn't need pensions. You had people to look after you, you had access to land to grow your own food, and the land was worked in harmony with nature so it could provide indefinitely. Small groups can be in touch with the laws and limits of nature while great bulging cities and urban sprawls cannot. This is where vast numbers in the Third World now live because they have been forced or encouraged off the land. There were also many sexual taboos that were passed on by the natural culture that also helped to limit population growth.

The Coca Cola culture that we have imposed on the Third World for our benefit and in our arrogance has shattered these societies and generated enormous confusion, fear, instability and insecurity. So they see their only salvation in more children who can work or beg or steal to scrape together enough to eat. In this way we achieve what you might think would be a contradiction: more poverty = more people.

Removing poverty and giving people back security and control over their own lives in small communities, self-sufficient in basic needs, is not just the way to eliminate hunger; it is the best way to stabilise the world population.

The emancipation of women

Women are central both to the problem and the answer. They do most of the work in these countries yet they are often treated as nothing more than baby machines. Even when food is short it normally goes to the men first, the children second and the women last of all.

Much more of our aid should be used to increase the status and education of women. They don't want to spend virtually their entire young lives pregnant, with all the effects that has on their health. They must be given the opportunities that will free them from this imprisonment. It is a woman's basic right to control her own fertility.

As a World Health Organisation report said: 'In developing countries women with no education have twice as many children as those with seven or more years schooling. The latter group is three times more likely to be using effective contraception.'

Family planning has a major part to play alongside education and social justice. The 1985 World Fertility Survey showed that: 'If most unwanted pregnancies in the Third World could be prevented it would reduce population growth in the less developed world by as much as 40 per cent.'

So there is no one answer because there is no one cause, though poverty and insecurity are at the core of it. The Green Party would work towards all these solutions both by direct aid and by influencing other countries through the European Community, the United Nations and the World Bank.

A population target for Britain

But let us not forget our obligations here at home. England is one of the most densely populated countries on Earth; it is no good people complaining about green land being lost to development while they see nothing wrong with a rising population. One is a consequence of the other.

Just ask where the fields would have been around your town or city 200 years ago and you will have one heck of a shock when you see the size of the area that has been built upon since then. An area of Britain the size of Berkshire, Buckinghamshire, Bedfordshire and Oxfordshire has disappeared under concrete since 1947. An area the size of a football pitch is concreted over every 20 minutes.

It can't go on, can it?

Not all the development has been caused by a rising population. Too much is done simply for profit with no benefit for the people as a whole. But once again it is obvious that as the population rises we will need more space to live and that means nature must give way. Our population is currently around 57 million and soon after we enter the next century it will have gone up another half a million.

There is great complacency about the British population because it has, by world standards, stabilised. But it is not stable. It is still growing. The system doesn't like slowly rising or stable populations because it wants more and more 'consumers'. I have heard industrialists explaining how bad it will be for business: I was almost moved to tears.

It is not, however, bad news for the youngsters who are competing with fewer people for the work available. There is even talk of companies being forced to treat their key workers much better to make sure they keep them. What a tragedy! Nor is it a problem for those looking for a place to live.

Therefore the Green Party believes we should aim for a steady reduction in the population of the United Kingdom to a sustainable level, which would in turn end our dependence on and exploitation of the poorest peoples of the world. We would set out to do this through education and information about the consequences of a rising population and the benefits of a slowly falling one. There would be a far greater expansion in family planning clinics and advice.

Greens are about the quality of life, not the quantity, and although the system would resist with everything it had, we are confident people would see the sense of smaller families. The environmental and human arguments are overwhelming.

Once again humankind has a choice to make. We can be sensible and limit our numbers voluntarily or we can go on until nature does it for us with disease and hunger. That will be deeply unpleasant for those around at the time . . . and the time isn't too far off.

As the eminent biologist, Sir Julian Huxley, said in 1945:

Somehow or other population must be balanced against resources or civilisation will perish. War is a less inevitable threat to civilisation than is population increase.

Since he said those words, the population of the world has doubled.

7: What's your poison?

Capitalism is the extraordinary belief that the nastiest of men for the nastiest of motives will somehow work for the benefit of all.
JOHN MAYNARD KEYNES

We are being poisoned by instalments. It is like a dripping tap day after day, yet there is no reason why this should have to be.

The politicians and their 'experts' will deny it. They will tell you there are safe levels of pesticides or additives or radiation, and the thousands of other poisons our bodies must absorb. This simply isn't true. Poisons are stored in the fatty tissues of the body and they build up over the months and years, affecting the natural chemical balance and causing cancer, birth defects, and many other serious and less serious health problems. Rachel Carson made this point as long ago as 1962 in her classic on pesticide poisoning, *Silent Spring*:

> When these reserves of fat are drawn upon the poison may strike very quickly. A New Zealand medical journal provided an example. A man under treatment for obesity suddenly developed symptoms of poisoning. On examination his fat was found to contain stored dieldrin, which had been metabolised as he lost weight. The same thing could happen with loss of weight in illness.

We can't measure what is a safe limit of exposure to these chemicals we face in our daily lives because of this build-up in the body. Don't let them persuade you otherwise.

The entire history of the subject is of politicians and experts assuring us we are in no danger, only for the next generation of politicians and experts to lower, sometimes drastically, the previous 'safe' levels of exposure. They told us DDT was safe, but many years, many poisonings, and much environmental damage later, they were forced to ban it. Rachel Carson said in 1962 that Aldrin 'projects a menacing shadow into the future . . .' It took 27 years for the authorities to admit she was right.

No bodies, no action

Remember how claims about asbestos were dismissed as 'alarmist', the usual official reaction to any protest? If that's true, how come they now close schools and other buildings when they remove asbestos? And why do the people who do it have to look like spacemen?

Answer: Because the government has seen the bodies. People have died horribly from the effects of breathing asbestos dust and the judgements of coroner's court after coroner's court have confirmed the connection.

When you point out the dangers of our poisoned world to the system that created it, the reply comes back: 'Oh yes? Then show me the bodies.'

No bodies. No action.

But the point they *deliberately* overlook is that because we are being poisoned bit by bit and not in one go, the cause and the result can be many years apart. In the end it can take a very small amount of exposure to push the body beyond endurance.

Once again, as with all Green Party policy, the solution is basic common sense. Forget about all the jargon they throw at you to fob you off. Is it not obvious that if the body is taking in levels, however small, of human-made poisons day after day which it has not evolved to cope with, and which are totally alien to it, then there are bound to be adverse effects? Yet the system asks us to believe the opposite, even though it is proved wrong with disgraceful regularity.

While we are forced to consume some of the poisons, the Earth gets the lot. In pesticides, in radiation, in industrial waste, in fossil fuel burning from power stations and cars. There is no hiding place. Traces of car exhaust gases and deadly chemicals like DDT have been found in the snow of the polar ice caps.

The danger from pesticides

People talk about living the healthy life in the country and eating fresh vegetables with lots of roughage for a healthy diet. Modern intensive farming is taking the 'health' out of both. Back in 1980, Edward Goldsmith said in *The Ecologist:*

> In the last thirty years there has been a veritable explosion in the use of synthetic organic pesticides. Over 800 formulations are now used in the UK alone. They include nematicides, fungicides, herbicides and rodenticides . . . Each of us has in our body fats, traces of hundreds of different pesticides.

Today the number of pesticides has passed a thousand and they make up more than 4,000 different products for use in farms, gardens, industry and homes. Between 97 and 99 per cent of the fruits, cereals and vegetables we eat are sprayed at least once by poison. In 1983 official figures revealed that one crop of lettuce had been sprayed 46 times with four chemicals; hops were dosed an average of 23 times a season; orchards 17; soft fruit and greenhouse vegetables more than eight; cereals at least three; arable crops like peas and potatoes just under five. The Association of Public Analysts found in the same year that a third of all fresh fruit and vegetables they tested were contaminated with pesticide residues.

Yet between 1983 and 1988 the area of land sprayed by these poisons went up by 30 per cent and farmers were paying £409 million for the privilege. Worldwide sales are worth many billions, with 2,500,000 tons produced every year.

And there you have the real reason why we are being subjected to this insanity. The giant companies who make the poisons make a fortune from their sale. Sensible farming methods, a clean environment and chemical-free food are not good for business.

The Ministry of Agriculture has always been close to the agro-chemical industry and its policies have reflected what is best for the industry rather than for the public it is supposed to represent. In the fifties they watered down or suppressed the recommendations in reports into pesticide dangers. They held off moves for control by law and instead introduced a voluntary code which was less than useless. They said that attempts to require registration of pest control firms to oversee their activities were 'an unwarranted interference with the freedom of commercial concerns.' They even changed the whole meaning of one report into the flimsy packaging of deadly poisons on the shelves of supermarkets and garden shops. The draft report said:

> We have been shocked by some of the containers in which toxic chemicals have been packaged and we consider with notable exceptions the standard of packaging to be generally well below that necessary for toxic substances.

When the civil servants got hold of it, the final version said:

> Although the standard of packaging generally is satisfactory, we deprecate the use of some containers in which toxic chemicals are packed.

This was just the start of more than 40 years of cover-ups, lies and mis-information by successive governments and civil servants to keep the truth about pesticide dangers from the public. The same goes for other poisons that pollute our world.

The results of all this have been quite, quite appalling.

When you spray something to kill a pest, it doesn't only kill the pest. It kills the creatures that eat the pest. It kills the creatures that come into contact with the crop. It kills the fish in the streams and rivers and it kills the birds that eat the fish. It kills friend and foe alike.

The book *Earth Report* tells the extraordinary tale of what can happen:

> Some years ago large quantities of DDT were used by the World Health Organisation in a programme of mosquito control in Borneo. Soon local people, spared the mosquito plague, began to suffer a plague of caterpillars which devoured the thatched roofs of their houses, causing them to fall in.
>
> The habits of the caterpillars limited their exposure to DDT, but predatory wasps that formerly controlled the caterpillars were devastated.
>
> Further spraying was done indoors to get rid of the houseflies. The local gecko lizards, which previously controlled the flies, continued to gobble their corpses — now full of DDT. As a result, the geckos were poisoned and the dying geckos were caught and eaten by house cats.
>
> The house cats received massive doses of DDT, which had been concentrated as it passed from fly to geckos to cat, and the cats died. This led to another plague, now of rats.
>
> They not only devoured the people's food, but also threatened them with bubonic plague. The government of Borneo became so concerned that cats were parachuted into the area in an attempt to restore the balance.

We interfere with nature's web at our peril.

If pesticides don't kill wildlife, they can stop them reproducing healthy off-spring or even any off-spring and, as with humans, they can damage their immune systems so making them open to diseases of all kinds.

There is endless evidence all over the world of how wildlife has been massacred in this way. The near extinction of the otter across England and Wales began in the 1950s and its decline is now known to have been caused in part by dieldrin poisoning. The population of butterflies, once so abundant, has been dramatically reduced by chemical and intensive farming. Yet they are actually allowed to spray this stuff from an aeroplane!

One British study showed that the children of agricultural workers, gardeners and groundsmen, have a well above-average rate of birth defects like spina bifida and there were 1,200 cases of children under four being poisoned by agro-chemicals in the home or garden in one year. A World Health Organisation survey found that human breast milk is seriously contaminated with pesticides and other chemicals – with enormous implications for the health of our children. It is now estimated that a million people are poisoned by pesticides each year with 20,000 deaths. This doesn't include the longer term health effects of pesticide contamination.

Friends of the Earth have compiled scores of cases in which people have had their health affected, some seriously, after being caught by spray drift, but the authorities always deny the link because they don't want the truth to come out – even now that the authorities in the United States have described pesticides as a 'major cause of cancer'.

We are not even allowed to know what tests have been done on these poisons before they are sold. Safety reports on pesticides registered before October 1986 are kept secret from the UK public. Reports on those registered after that can only be seen with ministerial approval. This is the attitude to public safety that allows 38 pesticides to be used in the United Kingdom that are banned or severely restricted in other countries. We also have 112 pesticides in everyday use that have not been tested since 1965 when the tests were far less stringent than they are even today.

It is quite astonishing. Politicians are elected to represent our interests, not those of the chemical industry.

What makes it so ridiculous is that all this is not necessary. What the poisons are trying to achieve can be done by biological control and other techniques which work with nature as nature intended.

If you have a pest you introduce a natural predator of that pest. It keeps the pest numbers down by feeding off them. The predators' numbers are kept in check by the number of pests available to feed them. You don't wipe out the pests, but then neither do the poisons. Indeed the latter are creating super-pests that have become resistant to the chemicals so more and more pesticides are needed to kill them. Where does it all end?

Food processing

We are not just being harmed by the way our food is produced on the farm. We have not yet mentioned the food processing industry.

Have you heard about the raspberry trifle that contains 27 additives and . . . no raspberry? That's the way the massive food processing companies and multi-nationals make their money at our expense.

Once again we come back to centralised production. No more than 45 distribution centres handle 80 per cent of our food, so to compensate for the length of time it takes to deliver long distances, they add preservatives. The longer the food can stay on the shelf when it gets there the more likely it is to be sold as well. With our policy of local production for local sale you wouldn't need to add those things in such quantities or even at all.

By the way, something you should know. The United Kingdom's definition of a preservative is 'any substance which is capable of inhibiting, retarding, or arresting the growth of micro-organisms, *or of masking the evidence of such deterioration.*' (My emphasis.)

They even add chemicals to our food to stop it sticking to

the processing equipment in the factory which, as a result, does not have to be cleaned so often. They are added to meat and frozen chickens to make them absorb water and so weigh heavier. You pay an awful lot of money for water when it comes to your chicken.

Monosodium glutamate is used in 15,000 processed foods. It is only there to stimulate our taste buds and kid us that the food has more flavour than it really has.

Ninety-nine per cent of the additives in our food are there for no other reason than to help sell the product. They are the colourings and the artificial flavourings. There are estimated to be more than 3,500 flavourings for the industry to choose from and they are subject to no proper regulations and no proper independent safety tests. Fewer than 350 additives of all kinds are regulated in the UK, no more than 10 per cent of those in widespread use. Even the tests for those are far from convincing. Yet again commercial interests come before public protection with the UK government.

Additives are allowed that are banned in some other countries and the technical reports prepared on this subject by the Ministry of Agriculture, Fisheries and Food come under the Official Secrets Act! Under no circumstances should the public be told what they are eating. Business might suffer. Profits might drop. Growth might be affected.

It is all money, money, money. The more food is processed, the more they add to it, the more they can charge for it. Only around 1p of the price of a packet of crisps is the actual potato.

The Green Party would end all this and the secrecy that allows it to happen. We would replace the present Ministry of Agriculture with a new Ministry of Food to put people's health and well-being before inflated profits for the few. We would end the use of unnecessary additives; those currently under particular suspicion would be withdrawn immediately. Anything added to food would be subject to thorough independent testing and the reports would be made public. Food would have to contain much more information on the percentage of the main nutrients, all additives, and all countries of origin.

Our policy is rather different from that of the UK government. In 1979 the Food Additives and Contaminants Committee listed 16 colouring additives for which evidence of safety was not available. Even so they recommended, and the government agreed, that these 16 additives could be used in food, but further evidence of safety was required within five years. That was in 1979. It took them until 1987 to clear them officially and even then, according to leading experts in this field, they used very dubious and complacent criteria. But, then, governments like being complacent. That is often the basis of their entire environmental policy. Complacency is good for economic growth.

Hazards in water

It is good for growth if you allow companies making gigantic profits to pour their waste into our rivers. Even the penalties for illegal dumping can be laughable. In 1981 a chemical company in Suffolk seriously polluted the River Stow with styrene and xylene, a substance linked with cancer. The river had to be cut off from the public water supply at one point, fish flesh was tainted, and the smell of the chemicals filled the town. The law came down hard. The company was fined £325.

The most awful poisons enter our rivers in the name of growth and international competition. The consequences for wildlife and the future never pass through the concrete that appears to stand between Westminster and reality.

It is this very attitude that is causing great concern about the water we get from the tap. Chemical farming has meant that vast amounts of nitrate fertiliser have been spread on the land, more than the growing crops can absorb. The unabsorbed nitrate is washed off the land into rivers and water supplies; or it soaks down into the ground water and off into the water supplies that way.

The nitrate levels in our water in some parts of the country are reaching alarming levels. When you think that it can take 20 years to filter down from field to ground water you can appreciate that worse is to come. We are now drinking nitrate residues which were spread on the land 20 years ago and we use far more today than we did then.

Excess nitrate can cause Blue Baby Syndrome because it affects the oxygen supply. Nitrate also becomes nitrite in the body which can combine with substances in food to produce an agent that has been linked with cancer.

Pesticides also get into the water supplies and yet few water authorities routinely test for them in any detail. Our water is contaminated by other chemicals that should never be there. We don't know what we are drinking and the authorities don't want us to know.

The Green Party would change this by forming an independent authority to control the quality of water. The large majority of its members would have no connection with the water or agro-chemical companies. The authority would be open to the press and its reports made public. Green farming policies would reduce nitrate applications immediately and considerably reduce concentrations in our water supplies in the longer term.

Disposing of waste

Now here's a figure to knock you back a bit (it did me, anyway!) Every year the world produces, and so has to dispose of, the best part of 400 million tonnes of hazardous waste, 90 per cent of which comes from the industrialised countries. How are the natural, and fragile, processes of nature supposed to survive that bombardment year after year? They can't, of course, and that's why they are in such decline.

It is very difficult to establish how much the UK produces because our policy is a shambles. It is reckoned to be between six and twelve million tonnes a year, to be disposed of in these small and densely populated islands.

Eighty-three per cent of it is dumped in land-fill sites – holes in the ground – with most of the rest poured into our rivers and seas. But even this has not been enough for the United Kingdom. We have been importing the stuff as well at the rate of about 190 tonnes a year.

You will not be surprised to know why we are so popular as a destination for this poisonous (though for some, highly profitable) trade. Our laws on waste disposal have been so lax or non-existent that many companies in this country have been able to offer cheaper deals than anywhere else and some of the stuff is so horrible that other countries are delighted to have some mug to take it off their hands.

The health of people and wildlife living near some of these dumps is in danger. The Green movement has been saying this for a long time and now even some governments are being forced to agree.

There are about 50,000 landfill sites in the United States, of which 20,000 are thought to be a threat to health. The cost of a clean-up operation, even if that's possible in some cases, was estimated by the Office of Technology Assessment at $100,000 million!

The West Germans have had to close 6,000 landfill sites as potential health hazards with 800 of those a threat to public water supplies. Clean-up costs: $10,000 million.

The Netherlands authorities were forced to act after a housing estate had to be evacuated because of a leaking dump. A survey of dumps was ordered and within six months 4,000 illegal dumps had been found. Clean-up cost: $1,500,000.

These are more of the hidden costs of growth economics that you are never told about when they measure economic 'progress'.

I'd like to tell you how many polluting dumps we have in the UK, but I can't. The Government has never bothered to find

out. A House of Lords Select Committee was told by representatives from the Atomic Energy Authority's Environmental Safety
Groups: 'We don't know how much hazardous waste is produced in the UK, who produces it, what it is, and what happens
to it.' This is irresponsibility on a gigantic scale. The committee
reported that we were living 'in a minefield for which we have
lost the chart.'

We are the only major industrial country in the EC not to
have carried out a survey of old waste dumps; yet every survey
so far conducted in Europe has revealed major environmental
and health hazards.

Market forces are at work again as waste operators ignore
the dangers to undercut the opposition. Once more we have a
situation in which it is cheaper to abuse people and the environment than to protect them. In this way, those companies who
are trying to do things properly have been undercut by the
cowboys. Cancer and other health effects or the contamination
of ground water supplies are subordinate to market forces.

The waste trade is now also turning its eyes to the Third
World. Even the regulations in this country won't apply there.
Either they will take it because they desperately need the money,
or deals will be struck with pay-rolled dictators, or the countries
simply will not be told what is going on. There is plenty of
evidence that this is happening already.

Sea dumping

Five million tonnes of sewage sludge and industrial waste, and
50,000 different chemicals, are dumped in the North Sea every
year. It is an open sewer. The North Sea is fast becoming a dead
sea. Faced with these facts the British Government calls the
North Sea 'a wholly healthy body of water' and has fought
tenaciously to block all attempts by other countries to clean it
up.

Britain is the only country disposing of sewage sludge in the

North Sea. Sewage can be used to make natural fertiliser for the land, but we allow industry to pipe its chemical waste into our sewage works and once the two are mixed the fertiliser option has clearly gone.

Southern Water also dumps around 250 thousand tons of this horrible mixture in the English Channel off the Isle of Wight every year. They have no idea what the long-term effects will be for marine life and indeed for humans. One survey showed that 40 per cent of flatfish in parts of the North Sea have cancer; a Dutch survey noted the increase in disease among flounders, dab and plaice with eleven per cent showing signs of liver cancer, ulcers and finrot; and chemical pollution is responsible for the loss of large numbers of eider, spoonbill, herring gull and tern. High rates of infertility, miscarriages, disease and weakened immune systems have devastated the seal population. One seal tested in Germany was found to harbour one thousand pollutants.

The whole marine food chain is contaminated by the poisons the industrial countries pour into the seas and who is at the end of the food chain? We are.

This pollution and over-fishing for short-term profit is threatening fish stocks all over the planet. Fish supply 23 per cent of the world's protein and provide a living for millions, but we treat them with such short-sighted contempt. The future of our marine food supply is under very serious threat. The Humber Estuary used to support a highly successful fishing industry, but no more. The chemical and industrial plants that have appeared along the estuary have killed it. The same thing on a bigger scale is happening to the North Sea and elsewhere and it is getting worse.

But then, we shouldn't worry. The government says it is 'a wholly healthy body of water.'

Radioactive waste

Mind you, they are just as optimistic about the Irish Sea – the most radioactive in the world. Which brings me on to the most disturbing contaminant of them all – radioactive waste.

Supporting the nuclear industry in all its forms is about as sensible as giving a three-year old a loaded gun to play with. There has always been natural radiation, but since the war radiation in the atmosphere has been increasing, substantially in some areas, as a result of nuclear weapons and nuclear power. Radioactive waste is routinely discharged into the atmosphere from all nuclear power installations every day.

Some substances, like plutonium, do not exist in the natural world. Plutonium is a by-product of nuclear power and an essential ingredient in most nuclear weapons. It is one of the most deadly poisons on Earth; the lethal dose is about one thousandth of a gramme.

Plutonium 239 has a half-life of 24,400 years, four times longer than recorded history. A half-life is the time it takes for a substance to halve its radioactivity and it's reckoned that 20 half-lives have to pass by before it returns to the level of natural background radiation. Therefore we must keep plutonium 239 isolated from people and the environment for around 500,000 years. That's worth bearing in mind when you consider that UK nuclear power stations in operation or under construction will produce 77.5 tons of plutonium. This to provide little more than *six per cent* of the energy used in this country by the most expensive form of energy generation ever invented. What's more, we even import other people's nuclear waste for re-processing.

We have no idea what we are going to do with the waste that is building up by the week, because every time the authorities try to choose a site the local people won't stand for it. Nor should they. A Yorkshire Television documentary about Sellafield (Windscale) found plutonium 239, americium 241, ruthenium

106 and caesium 137 in house dust at nearby Ravenglass. None of these things is found in the natural environment, but they are all involved in the nuclear industry. No wonder people want rid of nuclear power.

Radiation cover-ups

When government papers were released under the 30 year rule, we heard for the first time the truth about the Sellafield fire of 1957. We heard about the lies the public were told about the dangers. Many more cancer deaths and birth defects have been linked with that fire as a result of information kept from us all those years.

We now also know that the public were not told the truth about the dangers of the radioactive cloud that came over this country after the Chernobyl disaster. Meat was allowed to be sold that was way above even our 'safe' levels. Milk was consumed which should not have been. Independent surveys have shown levels of radiation in parts of Britain as a result of Chernobyl (and our own nuclear industry?) to be much higher than those claimed at the time by our government.

We were told the Chernobyl station did not have a containment building like British reactors to stop the radiation getting out, so the accident could not be repeated here. The truth was that Chernobyl did have a containment building. The explosion blew it to pieces.

They are swift to issue their 'no danger' propaganda, but they don't tell us that a leak at Sellafield went undiscovered for four years or that another released 100,000 curies of high-activity waste. They don't tell us about the fish caught in the Irish Sea contaminated with plutonium.

The truth is withheld because they don't want the public to demand an end to nuclear power. Rosalie Bertell (in her book, No Immediate Danger) catalogues an horrendous story of cover-up, secrecy, and lies, aimed at keeping the truth from the public throughout the world.

The effects of many hundreds of nuclear bomb tests since the 1950s have been denied even when painstaking research has revealed that soldiers at the test sites and people living nearby have died from similar cancers and diseases in numbers that have never occurred before.

One of the most appalling examples of official inhumanity was when the United States used the Marshall Islands for nuclear bomb tests in the fifties. Some people were forcibly moved from their homes to islands that could not support them while others were left to take the consequences of the fall out. Many have died or are still dying of cancer as a result. The people of Rongelap Atoll were evacuated three days after a bomb was tested there, but they were taken back with the island still ten times more radioactive than normal. An official memorandum gave away the reason why: 'The habitation of these people on the island will afford most valuable ecological radiation data on human beings.'

Such are the people in authority who shape our lives and ask us to trust them.

Preserving the balance of nature

I must keep stressing that nature is a delicate balance. If we disturb that balance, the effects could be disastrous. Oxygen, for instance, is around 21 per cent of the air we breathe. Any less and it would be too little, any more and it would be too much. If we can damage the ozone layer with chemicals that were supposed to be safe, will we come up with a chemical, or a cocktail of several, that will alter that oxygen balance?

It is this fragile balance that we must protect and respect at all times. Yet we go on as if nothing we do can harm it.

The relentless poisoning of our world is yet another area where green politics differs fundamentally from that of the grey parties. When there is a chemical spillage or accident, they demand that these poisons are used with greater care or moved around the country and the world more safely.

Our response is rather different: Why on Earth are we producing most of the stuff? We are told these substances are essential until they are shown to be highly dangerous. Then, apparently, we can get along fine without them.

The grey system always sees more science as the answer. Instead of stopping a course of action that is obviously dangerous, it has this immovable belief that science will find an answer.

The Green Party believes that the poisoning of the planet has become so serious that we must tackle it urgently. Not next year, not tomorrow, *NOW*. We don't have to poison ourselves: there is another way.

We would set up an Environmental Protection Commission to co-ordinate government policy, with enough inspectors to ensure that new pollution controls were followed. The number of inspectors employed today is laughable. They have got no chance of doing their job properly.

Polluters would pay the full cost of what they do. There would be pollution charges to pay for new waste treatment and disposal facilities; these charges would also act as an incentive to create less waste. The less pollution a company created, the smaller the charge. We would also make available capital grants for companies who wished to invest in pollution control, but there would be no subsidies for the cost of cleaning up the mess. If a company polluted the environment the fines would be designed to equal the full cost of the damage and the clean-up.

Once more we are turning the present system on its head and making it more economic to protect the environment than to poison it. Most companies will always be tempted to cut corners at the expense of the future if they are allowed, or even encouraged, to do so. We would remove that temptation. Companies would have to keep pollution control records in a format agreed by the Commission and inspectors would have powers to inspect accounts, statistics and waste disposal records. The secrecy has to stop so we can keep a record of what poisons are being produced and where they are going.

Private waste disposal contractors would be closely monitored by the local councils. Some of the outrageous behaviour that we see from some of the cowboy contractors would result in severe fines and the removal of licences.

Those chemicals with serious implications for the environment, like CFCs, would no longer be produced and all new chemicals would have to undergo rigorous tests to not only prove they are safe, but show that their use would be of real benefit to the community. Most chemicals already on the market and coming on the market today would fail that test.

The dumping of all toxic pollutants in rivers and seas would be ended. The most serious would be stopped immediately. The disposal of sewage sludge at sea would end. New laws would prevent the mixing of sewage and poisonous chemicals. This would allow the sewage to be turned into natural fertiliser which would be needed in greater quantities under Green farming policies.

The oil industry would have to provide tank cleansing facilities and no tanker would be allowed to leave port until this routine cleansing had been done. An enormous amount of oil pollution is caused by tankers washing out their tanks at sea. To reduce the chances of accidents involving chemicals, there would be stricter controls on the standard of ships and the competence of the crews. In the longer-term far fewer chemicals would be passing in and out of the country anyway.

We would decommission all nuclear power stations as quickly as possible, and all work on nuclear stations under construction would be stopped. Sellafield would be closed and all imports and exports of nuclear and other poisonous wastes would be ended. No ship carrying nuclear waste would be allowed to enter British territorial waters which extend twelve miles off the coast.

Putting policy into practice

Green Parties throughout the world thoroughly dislike words like 'ban', 'stop' and 'prevent'. The word we most like is *enable*, because our aim is to create the circumstances which enable people to control their own lives. But clearly if you allow companies the freedom to destroy, what does that do for the freedom of the rest of the population, the wildlife and all who must follow us? How can people control their own lives and destinies when they can't stop their own environment from being polluted?

Certain sectors of industry and business have shown themselves to be incapable of voluntary regulation because profit is put before everything, even human life. It is all short-sighted and short-term and the irresponsibility of successive governments has allowed them to get away with it. They leave us no choice but to introduce effective measures to protect people and the environment from their activities. They will claim that these new laws will make them uncompetitive in the world market – but that is one reason why the Green Party is committed to reducing our dependence on international trade and producing far more for ourselves.

Our pollution laws must be based on what is right for the environment and what is right for people, and not whether overseas companies can undercut us by polluting even more than we do.

We would act on the balance of probability. If there was any question of danger the substance or process would be banned. The onus would be on the company to prove beyond doubt that something was *safe* and not, as at present, on the public to prove beyond doubt that it was *dangerous*.

Public information is the key. The public can't make a proper choice at the moment because the facts are kept from us. We would have an environmental impact statement on all food and goods. If something was sprayed with chemicals, this would have to be declared and the chemicals listed. There would be public access to test reports. Sales would drop as a result and companies would have to find non-polluting, non-destroying alternatives, if they were to prosper. Once again it would become more economic to protect than destroy.

Instead of being the Dirty Man of Europe, a Green Britain would set the standard that others would, under pressure from public opinion, have to follow. Only by showing responsibility and commitment in these areas, only with truly Green values and principles, can we heal our sick and poisoned Earth.

8: The lie of the land

... live as though you will die tomorrow – but farm as though you will live for ever.
ANON

One of the most serious environmental problems facing us is the erosion and degradation of the soil.

Top soil is rarely more than a foot thick, often just a few inches, yet this is the base of all life on Earth. Without it there would be no plants, no animals, no us. You would think, therefore, that we would treat it with the reverence and respect it so clearly deserves. But we don't. We treat it like a factory floor.

It can take hundreds and sometimes thousands of years for nature to form an inch of top soil, depending on the land and the climate. Obviously, if the soil is eroded at a quicker rate than that, sooner or later it will disappear.

From soil to sand

A major factor in the collapse of the Roman Empire was this same process of abusing the soil to the point where it could not produce food. We all know what North Africa looks like today, but it wasn't always so. The wrong type of farming thousands of years ago did much of the damage and it has never recovered. Many civilisations have perished in this way. They over-used the soil to grow food for their expanding empires until the land was so degraded it could produce nothing. It is the same old story, more and more leading to less and less. Our problem now is that this is happening not only in one country, but throughout the world.

Official United Nations figures show that the Sahara Desert increases by an area the size of Czechoslovakia every decade, America has lost a third of its top soil since farming began there, and soil erosion in some of the poorest countries is at suicidal rates, caused by cutting down the forests and growing the wrong things on the wrong land in the wrong way for sale abroad. Global warming, the Greenhouse Effect, can only increase these pressures and we must address them immediately: the United Nations Environment Programme predicts that a third of the world's food growing land will be desert by the end of the century. Desert, by the way, doesn't just mean sand, but any barren land that cannot support adequate vegetation.

It is not that there are no answers to all this; there are, but the political will is missing as usual. Indeed for the last 40 years the politicians in Britain have taken us in quite the opposite direction, urged on by the agrochemical and drug companies, the National Farmers Union leadership, the farming press, and the big landowners of the type who see farming as merely a financial investment and not a way of life. When you think that the NFU is effectively run by the big landowners it is not surprising that an organisation that is supposed to support the interests of all farmers has promoted policies that have enriched the big and forced out the small.

Intensive farming and abuse of the land

There should simply be no soil erosion in Britain beyond the means of nature to replace it. The climate is on our side and it should not be a problem, but modern intensive farming has made it so with profound consequences for our children.

I saw shocking evidence of it one day on the Isle of Wight. After a night of heavy rain I was advised to go down to the River Medina and see the colour of it. It was like brown windsor soup, full of top soil being washed out to sea. In other areas, such as the grain-growing belts of East Anglia and elsewhere, the erosion rates are fantastic for a temperate climate. The Soil Survey estimates that, on average, Bedfordshire loses one tonne of soil per acre per year and this from fields that once had no erosion problems. It can be eleven tonnes an acre in the worst areas.

The supporters of intensive methods tell me that non-chemical farming can't feed the world. Recent US research shows this to be nonsense; and anyway the point they all miss is that their system definitely can't feed the world in the future because it cannot be sustained.

There was once a time when Britain had smaller, mixed farms which combined animals and crops. They were sustainable cycles in which the manure from animals was spread on the land (the old muck spreading) as a natural fertiliser and the fields were used in rotation so they could recover from the demands of growing arable crops. They would be rested for a time and sown with grass, which fed the animals. There was no problem with soil erosion, no need for artificial fertilisers and there were plenty of jobs for farmers and farm workers.

Then after the second world war came the race to produce as much as possible. This continued when we joined the European Economic Community which agreed to buy everything the farmers couldn't sell. If the public didn't want to buy because there was a surplus or the quality was poor, then the Common Agricultural Policy would pay up – and so we had the grain mountains and the wine lakes stored all over Europe or sold off at knock-down prices outside the Community.

It has not only been a ridiculous use of money, it has been a disaster for the soil, farm animals, the countryside, wildlife, and hundreds of thousands of small farms that were forced out of business. This all came about because to make more money you had to use more land, every inch if possible, and it became an incentive to destroy and introduce the bleak, soulless prairies that parts of this country have become.

Since 1947, 140,000 miles of hedgerows have been pulled up, much of them thanks to government grants. This has allowed farmers to make fields bigger to plant more crops and use the giant modern machinery. Uprooting the hedges means removing the habitat of large numbers of animals and insects.

Most of our magnificent wetlands, some of the finest and most beautiful in the world, have been drained and destroyed to plant more land for crops that no one could sell, except to the Community. Again much of this drainage was supported by government grants and again wildlife has suffered massively. We have also lost 95 per cent of our flower rich meadows, 60 per cent of lowland heath, and 50 per cent of ancient lowland woods – all in little more than forty years.

The British countryside has been devastated by these farming policies. I've seen many places designated Areas of Outstanding Natural Beauty that are nothing of the kind any more because they have become great wastelands of one-crop farming. Other European countries have not been as hysterical as we have in the race for more production at all costs. You can see in France and Germany for instance how this country used to be, with abundant hedgerows, smaller fields, and endless forests and copses.

To increase yields have come the nitrates and other artificial fertilisers plus the pesticides, herbicides and fungicides with all the hazards for food, water, farmworkers and those who live in the countryside. It has made agro-chemical companies even richer and it has made a fortune for the big landowners, but the price we are all paying for that in soil damage alone is immeasurable.

Soil is not just dead matter, or at least it wasn't until modern farming took over. It is made up of billions of minute organisms and bacteria which form the new soil and keep it healthy. If the pesticides don't kill these creatures then the herbicides will kill the vegetation that feeds them, which has the same effect. Worms and insects are killed by the poisons and yet they are vital to a healthy soil. Charles Darwin said of worms: 'It may be doubted whether there are many other animals which have played so important a part in the history of the world as have these lowly organised creatures.' So not only are we eroding the soil at rates well beyond its capacity to re-form, we are reducing its ability to re-form at all.

Removing the hedges and tree cover is making the soil more prone to wind erosion and, the biggest threat in British farming, erosion by water. Trees and hedges not only stop water having a free run across exposed land, they also absorb some of it. Today's giant farm machinery is so heavy it compacts the soil and creates wheel gulleys. This stops the rain penetrating the surface and allows the water to run away, taking top soil with it. This action is encouraged by planting the same crop one after the other without a break or use of organic fertiliser, thus reducing the organic content of the soil until it ceases to bind together. The move to winter crops leaves the land ploughed and exposed in periods of high rainfall. The guaranteed buying encouraged farmers to bring low quality land into arable production and hillsides have also been ploughed with obvious results for erosion. Even worse, the big, cumbersome, modern machinery makes it too difficult and dangerous to plough around the hills which would reduce erosion. Instead they have ploughed up and down the slopes which creates just about the worst erosion of all. The causes of our disappearing soil are many, but the common denominator is modern farming methods and policies that encourage them.

Yes, you can blame those farmers who jumped on the gravy train without a thought for the future; and you can certainly blame those who came into farming simply to invest their money for the biggest return in exactly the same way they would in the stock market. They are not farmers, but agro-businessmen: agriculture can do without them. But for every farmer you can point the finger at, you can find many more who are casualties of the system. The Samaritans say farmers are twice as likely to commit suicide as other groups. Why should this be if the system is working?

Farmers were guaranteed a buyer for their produce, but the price in real terms was falling because there was such a surplus. The only way farmers could compensate for this was to cut costs and increase production, but of course the smaller farms soon reached the limits of both and were swallowed up by the big boys and the agro-businesses. As the poisons, ever larger machinery, and intensive animal systems took over from farm workers, so came the collapse of country life and employment. One of the saddest results of all this was that most of those forced off the land were the very people who understood the limits of nature and how to farm within them.

It was the end of the war that the Labour government with all-party support launched the race for growth in farming production. You could understand it in the mood of the time with rationing and the threat to our food supplies during the war, but it has turned into a monster. In 1945, there were half a million farmers and around a million farm workers. There are now little more than 200,000 farms and the number of workers is a fraction of what it was.

This has had a terrible effect on rural employment. People have had to seek work in the towns and cities adding to the already immense pressures there, while commuters have moved into the villages and sent house prices soaring well beyond the locals' ability to buy.

All this has happened because of short-sighted, live-for-today farming policies perpetuated by politicians who have failed to see the human and environmental mayhem they have left in their wake.

Now, with the politicians cutting back on the Common Agricultural Policy, we have quotas and other limits on production which are leaving many farmers in severe financial trouble. They borrowed so much to expand in the good times and they can't meet the payments as their incomes fail to keep pace. The latest we are told is that farmers must take land out of production and turn it to other uses when 125,000 acres go under concrete in the UK every year as it is. What a gigantic mess they have created and it's as far from reality as you can possibly get.

Let us return to the real world, shall we?

A green farming policy

Today's farming is dependent on inputs based on finite resources which are at the mercy of price fluctuations, especially as supplies diminish or get harder to extract. It takes around two tons of oil to produce one ton of nitrate fertiliser. Even the pound of tomatoes you buy from the shop will have taken the energy equivalent of two litres of petrol to grow. We can't go on wasting all these resources and causing all this pollution just to increase the profits of the agro-chemical companies.

It is up to the politicians to provide the structure and support to break farmers' dependency on irreplaceable resources and highly expensive machinery. Failure to do so will have alarming effects on the future costs of farming and food.

There was once a time when farms were virtually self-sufficient. Almost everything that was needed to run the farm you could find on the farm. Not so today. Farmers could not operate without buying in most of what they need, and in fact around 60 per cent of their work is dependent on imported resources. Clearly this cannot be defended when you think of the damage, cost, and dependency on imports that results from it.

The Green Party's agriculture and countryside policies would restore this near self-sufficiency to our farms. It is not a case of going back. Technology and know-how have moved on, but, as I've said before, they have been misdirected. If we apply this know-how to another kind of farming and fund research to increase our knowledge further, then we can protect the land

and produce high yields. Again it has been lack of political will that has been holding us back. Today all the research is aimed at chemical farming while the organic farmers get no such support. Even so, the leading organic farms which have had years of experience are getting comparable yields in many cases to the average from the chemical variety. I met an ex-employee of ICI at the Royal Show one year who told me that with properly funded research there was no doubt that organic farms could produce as much as the average chemical yield does today (but won't tomorrow if the soil is lost and degraded).

Look at the advantages of organic agriculture: it doesn't cause serious erosion; it restores and replenishes the soil by mixing free-range animals with crops so the manure can be returned to the land as a natural fertiliser; it doesn't contaminate food and the soil with chemical sprays and artificial fertilisers; it saves the farmer the horrendous and increasing cost of buying those things; it is more labour-intensive so bringing back life and employment to the countryside; it will leave our children a land that can feed them.

Organic farming works with nature at all times. Pests are kept down by introducing the natural predator to maintain a balance to stop the pest population getting out of control. There are other controls like breeding varieties of crops that are resistant to pest attack. Weeds are controlled by simply pulling them up (some of the older organic farms in Europe have developed small-scale machinery to make this quicker and easier) and by rotating crops so the weeds never have long to establish themselves.

It is not as easy as looking on the side of a bag and reading the instructions, but all the farmers I have met who have stepped off the chemical treadmill are thoroughly enjoying the new challenges of organics, and they get great satisfaction from it.

Protecting the farmers

The Green Party will take British farming in this direction by using our subsidies to encourage organics and discourage chemicals.

Our policy of income support is a crucial departure from the present system. It will give farmers a decent income without encouraging them to produce more than the land can stand at the expense of the soil, natural beauty and wildlife. It will not encourage wasteful surpluses which can be dumped on the Third World. It is this guaranteed buying, known as price support, which has fuelled intensive agriculture and caused so much damage. Green policies, based on income support, will discourage all these practices.

Farmers, farmworkers and their families would receive their Basic Income. There would also be grants to cover the loss of income in the three years it takes to convert from chemical to organic farming and there would be our Farm Compensation Scheme which would be a subsidy to existing farmers who face a serious drop in income with the abolition of guaranteed buying by government. It would only be paid to those farming at the time guaranteed buying was abolished.

We would also introduce our voluntary Farm Revenue Stabilisation Scheme to even out the annual and seasonal fluctuations in farm incomes. Farmers could, if they wished, join an insurance scheme for the whole or part of their land for any period they liked. The scheme would, for example, set a national average income per hectare for a future harvest. If the income turned out to be less than the average predicted, the farmer would be paid the difference. If it turned out to be more, the farmer would pay the scheme the difference. Over a period, the scheme would pay for itself, farmers would enjoy more stability of income and so more long-term security against fluctuations in weather and yields.

It is wrong to expect farmers to be the unpaid conservers of the countryside for the rest of society. There would be grants and payments to encourage the restoration of hedgerows, wildlife habitat, wetlands, and traditional trees and forests. This is in fundamental contrast to the system which has given grants to destroy most of these things and encourage the conifer plantations which acidify the soil and look so awful in their regimented rows. I call them the silent forests, such is the absence of birdsong and wildlife.

Payments will be given for agricultural and conservation improvements if farmers produce a comprehensive Farm Development and Conservation Plan which would be approved by a public conservation agency. This allows the community to have a say in the development of the countryside and how their money is spent. The present Wildlife and Countryside Act is like trying to stop a tank with a pop gun and in terms of protecting wildlife and the countryside it has been a disaster. We will strengthen it by extending habitat protection to the whole countryside, not just a few selected areas. Species protection will be tightened and vigorously enforced. In the longer term we will not need designated National Parks or Areas of Outstanding Natural Beauty because all the countryside will be treated with equal respect.

Access to land

The Green Party is determined to give far more people access to farming and we would therefore limit the amount of farmland anyone could own. In Denmark, there is an upper limit on farm holding of 200 hectares and it cannot be owned by an absentee landlord or a big institution – as much of British farmland is. We favour limits on land value. This means that the limits will be lower on the fertile land which can produce a good income, but higher in, say, upland areas where you need more land to make a decent living. The highest rates of subsidies and grants in all their forms would go to smaller, less wealthy farms, as long as they worked the land within natural limits. Farming methods that cause irreparable damage to the land would be penalised. Central to Green values is that the land cannot be 'owned' by individuals so they can do what they like with it, irrespective of its effect on present and future generations. Our lives are but tiny episodes in time and we are under an obligation as a community to hand over that land in good condition to those who follow us.

It is a basic Green principle that all people should have access to fresh, healthy, locally grown food whatever their income. Today the poorest are often forced to buy additive-infested rubbish. We would subsidise if necessary the price of fresh, non-chemical food grown locally for local consumption so everyone could afford to buy it.

Local food co-operatives would be encouraged to co-ordinate local production and distribution. There would be a system of subsidies and tariffs to make local production cheaper or at least no dearer than imported produce of the same type and there would be curbs on the power of the food processing industry which currently controls, in effect, the entire food chain from ploughing to plate.

Before the system reels back in horror at this use of public money, hold on a second. Food production today is subsidised to an enormous degree through things like guaranteed buying, the storing of surpluses or their sale at low prices to other countries, and all the costs of cleaning up pollution caused by modern farming, the damage to the soil, the damage to health, contamination of drinking water and the waste of finite resources. The Common Agricultural Policy costs the average family between £11 and £13 a week even before you add all those other costs.

For that you get a devastated countryside and alarming soil erosion, farmers leaving the land in their thousands, a farm going into liquidation in the European Community every two minutes, the dismantling of traditional rural communities, agriculture dependent on expensive chemicals and fertilisers, and unhealthy food.

Switch your money to what the Green Party is proposing and you get none of those things. What you do get is fresh, healthy, staple foods that everyone can afford, produced locally for local sale. If you make chemical food production pay all the costs it is responsible for, you will see that organic farming is the most cost-effective way to produce our food as well as being the healthiest.

Two other things we would encourage are the development of the agricultural system called permaculture and research into the use of human sewage as land fertiliser.

Permaculture was a term coined by an Australian, Bill Mollison, to describe the system of farming and growing that combines plants, animals, buildings, water, and the local landscape in a way that produces more energy than it uses, re-cycles all nutrients and materials, and interferes with nature as little as possible. For some crops the soil isn't even turned over. The support for permaculture is gaining momentum fast, especially in Australia and the United States, and it has great potential for everyone using the land, whether gardener or farmer. I believe it will play an increasing role in Green Party farming policy in the years ahead.

Turning human sewage into farm fertiliser may sound peculiar on first hearing, but what is the difference between that and animal manure? One of the ways in which human beings break the natural cycle is that instead of returning our waste to the land as fertiliser like animals do, we pour it into the rivers and seas. We have turned what should be an important natural resource into a colossal pollution problem that costs a fortune to deal with even under Britain's lax regulations. It is only commonsense to investigate ways of using this resource in a useful way and, at the same time, removing or reducing the problems and costs of the current methods of disposal. Would you rather natural fertiliser on the land or sewage on the beach?

It is important that we fund research into a variety of natural fertilisers because of the implications for animal rearing in the long term. I believe meat and dairy consumption will fall substantially in the future as the public realise the consequences of it for health and for starving people.

Animals on the farm

I have so far only briefly mentioned farm animals, because they deserve special comment. Of all the victims of modern farming it is the animals who have suffered, and continue to suffer, the most.

When we had small mixed farms the animals lived out on the land in the fields which were resting after their spell under arable crops. It was all part of the eco-system. However, when intensification came along it had two main effects. First, we had farm specialisation with some areas concentrating totally on arable and crop production and others on meat and milk. This immediately divorced the natural manure fertiliser from the arable land with some results I've already described on the soil. It also meant that the big intensive animal farms produced more manure – or slurry, as it is called – than they know what to do with and too much of this can also cause severe pollution to rivers, streams and water supplies. So you have a situation in which the arable farms now pollute with chemicals and the animal farms with slurry: slurry can be 100 times more polluting than human waste, and silage 200 times! We have taken a solution and neatly divided it into two problems.

But for the animals, it is far worse than that. In the race to produce more meat, eggs and milk in the quickest time on the smallest amount of land came the factory farms. Most people will have seen the chicken sheds that together house 500 million chickens in this country. The appalling conditions kill between 20 and 30 million of them every year even before they can be taken to the horrors of the slaughter house. They spend their tragic 'lives' standing on wire mesh in an area not much bigger than this piece of paper. The behaviour problems that must result from that lead to them tearing at each other with their beaks, or even to cannibalism. What is farming's answer? To put them in humane conditions? No, to cut their beaks. They do it by cutting through the tissue as sensitive as the quick of a human nail.

The only aim of modern farming is to get animals as fat as possible as quickly as possible on the smallest possible amount of food. There is no thought for the animals as living creatures with feelings and emotions. They are just lumps of meat to be fed growth-inducing drugs, and prevented from running around. Every time they run, they use calories and we can't have that! Calories mean cash.

Take those little furry chicks that the children love. You can't help but say 'aah' when you see them. Well, 'aah' might not be quite the word that comes to mind when you hear that each year around 40 million of them are gassed at a day old for the unforgivable crime of being male. You may have seen the pathetic pictures of these creatures within hours of arriving in the world travelling down a production line conveyor belt. At one point there is an exit and if they are male and the wrong breed that's where they go. To die.

The genetic engineers have produced two types of chicken. There are those bred for the shops which get fat very quickly on the minimum of food and there are those bred to lay as many eggs as possible, again on the minimum of food. So if you are one of the latter breed and you are male you have had it. You can't lay eggs and you can't put on weight fast enough to be 'economic' and your time on this Earth lasts no more than 24 hours.

Actually, I say they are gassed. Many are, but others can be suffocated or have their skulls crushed. There is no law to say how they are killed. Every time people buy factory farm eggs and chickens they are supporting this evil trade whether they like it or not.

Pigs are accepted as intelligent animals and it is impossible to contemplate the agony they go through with their treatment on the factory farms. 400,000 sows in Britain are kept for most of their lives, sometimes all their lives, in stalls that allow them to stand up or lie down – nothing else. They are lined up in the so-called 'rape-rack' for conception and then in the shortest possible time after giving birth, it all happens again. Once their bodies are wrecked so they can produce no more, off they go to slaughter. Their babies are taken away from them soon after birth to be fattened up and in little over 20 weeks they are slaughtered, often without even feeling the sun on their backs and certainly not the joys of life.

The basic natural bond between mother and baby in all species is denied throughout the factory farm system. We are led to believe it doesn't matter because they are just dumb animals who don't understand these things. Such views are an insult to the intellect.

Mark Gold, one of Britain's leading campaigners for animal justice, tells the story of a heifer called Blackie in his book, *Living Without Cruelty*. In December 1983 her eight-week-old calf was taken from her at market and sold to another farm. In the middle of the night Blackie got out of her field and walked seven miles through Devon lanes until she found her calf. Dumb? Don't understand? The senses of animals are highly developed and this knowledge just adds to the horror of what we do to them.

But this horror is not only present on the farms. *Every week* in Britain we slaughter eight million chickens, 300,000 pigs, 80,000 cattle, 500,000 turkeys, 50,000 rabbits and 300,000 sheep. It is carried out in conditions which, if every person could see them, would destroy the meat industry overnight.

In 1984, the government's advisory committee on the subject gave 40 slaughterhouses prior warning of their inspection and yet still found animal cruelty wherever they looked. The animals are routinely given electric shocks to make them go in the required direction when the animals can sense the terror ahead from the noise and smell. They are then taken to the 'stunning' areas where they are supposed to be made unconscious before having their throats cut. As the report said: 'The unconsciousness and insensibility are being assumed to exist in many slaughtering operations when it is highly probable that the degree is insufficient to render the animal insensitive to pain.'

This was especially true for pigs, sheep and some calves; as Mark Gold puts it, 'As a result, many animals are probably fully conscious when shackled by the back leg and hoisted on the slaughterline to have their throats cut.'

Adult cattle are killed by the captive bolt pistol which fires a three-and-a-half inch bolt into the brain, but Dr. Gerlis, a consultant pathologist from Leeds, pointed out: 'It is a horrifying fact that approximately one-third of the cattle shot in this way are not stunned, but stand grieviously wounded and fully conscious while the pistol is re-loaded.'

Chickens go to their deaths hung upside down on a conveyor chain. They are dragged through a water bath charged with low voltage electricity. Often the birds lift their heads and are not stunned. An automatic knife then slits their throats, but the very small or large hens will be cut in the breast or head instead.

The slaughterhouses are true disciples of the system. They are only interested in throughput with the workers paid by the number of animals they kill. What are we doing having the audacity to call ourselves civilised when we allow this to go on in our names. We are all diminished by what is done and so we should be. As someone once said: 'If the walls of the slaughterhouses were made of glass, we'd all be vegetarians.'

Our system makes money out of every inch of every animal. Everything from the nostrils to the tail is used somewhere in the food processing industry or turned back into animal feed. This is one reason why disease is spreading through the food industry and the drugs fed to animals to make them fatter or calm them down in their outrageous conditions are helping to create super-bacteria that are resistant to drug treatment. As always we will get paid back with interest for this barbarism.

The threat from BSE

The brain disease bovine spongiform encephalopathy (BSE) has already been passed on from sheep to cattle by using sheep remains in cattle feed and there is great concern that it can be passed on to humans. There are many other real and potential risks to human health in the way we treat our animals and food.

But still the system goes on floating on its cloud of unreality as if nothing was wrong. We genetically engineer our animals so they become milk or meat machines a world away from what nature intended. Now we have the hormone known as BST to increase milk yields in already over-stressed, over-worked cows.

The drug manufacturers say it is safe for humans and so does the Secretary of State for Agriculture, but the committee advising the government on its safety is barred by law from telling the public if we are being told the truth. Independent scientists on the committee have been threatened with prosecution if they talk about the dangers of drinking milk produced in this way. We are now governed in such a sinister fashion that press releases about the committee's discussions on the subject were written and agreed by government and drug companies even before the advisory committee had met to discuss it!

But then, as I keep stressing, government departments work on behalf of powerful interest groups like the drug and agrochemical industries and not the people they are supposed to represent. To have one government department, the Ministry of Agriculture, Fisheries and Food responsible for both the companies that produce and the people who consume is clearly a serious conflict of interests – hence the Green Party's commitment to a Ministry of Food that would put people and animals first. It is also not surprising when you see how the system treats farm animals, allows blood sports, and kills millions of creatures needlessly in experiments, that the Green Party would have a minister for animal welfare to ensure these terrible practices were stopped.

There are many who still believe there is a difference between the abuse of animals and the abuse of people. There isn't. The two are indivisible. Tethered pigs and nuclear weapons may not seem to have any connection whatsoever, but they have. Both are created by the same state of mind.

It was summed up by Henry Salt, an environmentalist and social reformer who died in 1939. He said:

> Reformers of all classes must recognise that it is useless to preach peace by itself, or vegetarianism by itself, or kindness to animals by itself. The cause of each of the evils that afflict the world is the same – the general lack of humanity, the lack of the knowledge that all sentient life is akin, and that he who injures a fellow being is in fact doing injury to himself. The prospects of a happier society are wrapped up in this despised and neglected truth, the very statement which will, at the present time (I well know) appear ridiculous to the accepted instructors of the people.
>
> As long as man kills the lower races for food or sport, he will be ready to kill his own race for enmity. It is not this bloodshed, or that bloodshed, that must cease, but all needless bloodshed – all wanton affliction of pain or death upon our fellow beings.

How right he was, but what would he think today? I also recall a great line by George Bernard Shaw: 'Animals are my friends. I don't eat my friends.'

Eating meat causes hunger

I became a vegetarian after reading about the way farm animals are treated and I immediately gained by being introduced to a magnificent range of new foods I didn't know existed and by an improvement in my health and sense of well being. Meat and dairy products are among the great food killers of our age.

But not eating meat and, if you are a vegan, avoiding dairy products, is not just about health and animal abuse. I keep talking about connections and here's one of the most important of all. The connection between hungry children and eating meat. We are spun the yarn that we increase agricultural production with chemicals and poisons in order to feed people. No we don't. We increase agricultural production to feed farm animals – to grow meat or, if you own a company involved in meat or dairy production, to grow money.

It is hard to believe, I know, but it's true just the same, that only *eight per cent* of our farmland in Britain is growing crops for consumption by people. The rest is for animal feed. What was that they said about not being able to feed people without chemicals? It has been estimated that this country could feed a population of 250 million on an all-vegetarian diet without any food imports. We have around 57 million.

Turning grain into meat is incredibly wasteful. You have to feed an animal on average ten pounds of vegetable protein to create one pound of meat protein. It takes five acres to provide protein for one person for a year from meat while in the same area you can provide the yearly protein for three people from wheat and 30 people from soya. An organic vegetarian system of food production would also save other resources. In a world of scarce and diminishing water supplies, it takes 60 gallons of water to produce a pound of wheat, yet a pound of meat needs . . . 2,500 gallons. Even a quarter of the fish caught every year end up in farm animals.

This waste of protein and land is bad enough in this country, but it can be a death sentence on the poor throughout the less developed world. We actually import crops grown in countries where there is widespread hunger in order to feed our farm animals and boost the profits of the meat and dairy industries. Only a system motivated by greed and not need could sanction this obscenity.

In 1984 during the Ethiopia famine Britain imported £1.5 million worth of feed from there to give to our farm animals. More than a third of the crops produced in the world are fed to livestock while over half a billion people are severely malnourished. The European Community is one of the biggest importers of animal feeds with nearly 15 million hectares of the Third World growing food for European livestock, including Britain. The multi-nationals have taken over vast areas of these countries to grow animal feed for the West while people go hungry in those same areas for the want of land. These are the things we have to take into account when we survey the steak or hamburger on our plates.

Mind, you'll never guess the latest. They are selling factory farm technology to hungry countries and encouraging them to produce food in this way. I had better not write what I'm thinking at this moment.

The system that abuses farm animals *and* feeds them at the expense of hungry people has only survived, as always, because the connections have been hidden and kept from the public. The Green Party would make those connections clear; the public could then make a truly informed choice on what they wanted to eat.

So as you have seen, Green farming is heading in the opposite direction from what we have today. It will mean more hedges, traditional trees, wetlands, and natural beauty. It will bring stability and security for farmers, more jobs on more farms, and revitalise the rural economy. Animals will be treated with respect and as fewer people choose to eat meat and dairy products, the use of animals for food will diminish and the use of other people's land to feed them will end as soon as possible. Artificial fertilisers and the poisonous sprays would be phased out, and the soil would be worked only within its capacity to recover. Wildlife would flourish and nature would be a friend, not an enemy.

It will be a civilised agriculture for a civilised society.

9: Save and survive

If you take a frog from its pond and put it in a pan of hot water, it will jump out. If you put it in a pan of cold water and heat it slowly on the stove, the frog will sit there until it boils to death. The frog's senses are equipped to measure only large differences in temperature, not gradual ones.

Today, the human race has a lot in common with the frog in the pot.

THE NEW SCIENTIST

The energy policies pursued in the United Kingdom should be a national scandal. Irresponsibility and inefficiency over so many years in this country and throughout the developed world are now threatening to change the climate in a way never previously experienced in human history.

Global warming

Global warming – the 'greenhouse effect' – allows the sun's rays in, but stops much of that heat from escaping again. It traps it around the Earth so the temperature rises. It is impossible to say how much the temperature will increase, but it is thought that by the year 2030, well within our children's lifetimes, it will rise by between 1.5 and 4.5 degrees above pre-industrial levels; and that is only the start. It may not sound much, but when you think that if the temperature dropped by five degrees we would be in an ice age, you can see the immensity of the change we will have to cope with.

When temperature has changed in the past, when we went into and out of the last ice age, this happened over many thousands of years and living things had the chance to adapt slowly to the changing circumstances. Some couldn't and so died out, but most could and survived.

Today's climatic change is happening not over thousands of years, but over little more than 200. The change will be so swift that many forms of life will not be able to adapt in time and they will be lost forever.

Nor will the changes in temperature be consistent. The polar regions will be most affected and a three degree average temperature rise could mean an increase at the poles of around eight degrees. As the ice melts so the sea levels will rise and unthinkable amounts of money, perhaps impossible amounts, will be needed to protect many of the world's major cities, including London, while low-lying areas of the Earth will disappear under water. The atolls of the tropics will disappear in the next 30 years, according to some experts, making their peoples homeless, and releasing into the water the large amounts of radioactivity from the underground nuclear weapons tests that have taken place in some of them.

The climate is likely to change to the point where many of today's major grain growing areas – including the U.S. – will no longer be able to produce grain, or at least not enough for export.

There will be extremes of weather with years of drought followed by years of floods in some areas. Disasters like the hurricane force winds that wreaked such damage in southern England some years ago are likely to be more frequent.

It would be the understatement of all time to say global warming is serious. We have waited so long for action already, some 40 to 50 years too long, that some of the consequences are unstoppable. What we can do is limit the scale, but we must act quickly.

The main heat-trap gases are CFCs (including the ozone-friendly variety), methane, and the most significant at the moment, carbon dioxide. This comes mostly from burning tropical forests or any plant life, from vehicle exhausts, and from burning fossil fuels in our power stations.

This is one of the many reasons why the burning of the rain forests is so dangerous for all of us. Trees remove carbon dioxide from the air and store it safely (as wood) where it can do no harm. But when you burn the trees all that carbon built up over so long is released into the atmosphere. Imagine then, the amount of carbon dioxide set free in this way when an area of tropical forest the size of England and Wales is destroyed each year.

Intensive agriculture which uses far more fossil fuels than our organic approach is also adding to global warming by producing carbon dioxide and methane on a much greater scale than necessary.

The expansion in road vehicles is making the greenhouse effect far worse (I'll go into detail about transport in Chapter 10) but for now let us concentrate on another crucial area, power generation.

Energy policies

Yet again we are messing with nature's natural balance. We need to have a limited greenhouse effect. Without carbon dioxide in the atmosphere to trap some of the sun's heat the Earth would be a very cold and unpleasant place indeed.

Nature had the balance right until the industrial revolution. The carbon dioxide and other gases that industrialism has produced at such a fantastic rate have pushed nature off balance to a degree that could threaten life itself.

The situation is this. Burning fossil fuels is warming up the Earth, so we have to burn much less. It *can* be done without nuclear power and without anyone sitting in a freezing cold home – as so many do today despite our shocking waste of energy. What we *can't* do is continue as we are.

Despite the desperate need to reduce fossil fuel burning, we throw away more heat from our power stations every year than is generated by the entire production of North Sea gas every year.

Converting fossil fuels into electricity is incredibly inefficient the way it is done today. Less than 40 per cent of the energy released by burning fossil fuels is converted into electricity and another eight to ten per cent is lost in the transmission and distribution of electricity. Most of the potential heat is poured into the sky as flue gases and steam. The system sees what could be a valuable resource merely as waste. The Green Party wants to use this 'waste' steam by putting it into pipes to heat homes and workplaces. This would mean those homes and workplaces currently burning fossil fuels and creating pollution to provide their heat would no longer have to do so. The 'waste' would do it instead. To do this we have to phase out the giant power stations and replace them with smaller combined heat and power stations. They have to be smaller because the waste heat can only travel so far before it begins to cool. Again small proves to be more efficient. Combined heat and power stations have shown this where they have been introduced abroad.

One of the main reasons that combined heat and power is not in widespread use in this country is that we have different organisations for different forms of power. So the people who run electricity are obsessed with generating and selling electricity. They don't think in terms of energy, just energy via electricity. Hence steam is seen as waste and not potential heat because you can't plug it into the national grid.

The gas people are the same. They are only interested in selling gas and the products that use gas, and they enter into wasteful competition with electricity and other forms of energy.

What we need is not competition between energy sources, but their most efficient use. The right energy source for the right job. It is enormously wasteful to use electricity for space heating, yet we see advertisements all the time telling us that we should use it to heat our homes. They don't mention that to do so you will be wasting scarce resources and creating yet more unnecessary pollution when another form of energy would do it better.

We would end this competition by combining the gas and the electricity industries under a new Central Energy Authority which would have the task of promoting the use of the various fuels in the most appropriate way on the basis only of efficiency. This authority would also set up District Energy Authorities where the main decisions would be made. It would be their job to use all forms of energy available in their area on the basis of what wastes the least and creates the least pollution. We should be looking at what assets individual communities have and using those assets in the most effective way.

The Green Party would create energy eco-systems wherever possible in which a process makes its own energy to power the process. One example is of sewage gas being used to power a sewage works without the need to take from the grid. Similarly, we would encourage farms to use farm wastes, where possible, to reduce the amount of power they need to take from outside; rubbish that could not be recycled, but could be burned safely, would be burned to create energy; and those landfill sites we do have would be tapped, again where possible and appropriate, to produce land-fill gas. All these sources of energy and more are used around the world, but they can only be used in a small-scale way. There are so many sources of energy going to waste because the industry is too big and profit-driven to encourage and develop them.

The prime examples of this are the clean, unlimited sources of energy like wind, wave and solar power which have been starved of development and research funding. So has geothermal energy which uses the natural heat from underground. According to the Friends of the Earth booklet, *Energy Without End*, geothermal heat could have tremendous potential:

Within the top 10 kilometres of the Earth's crust at depths

accessible with current drilling techniques, there is sufficient heat to meet all the UK's energy needs for hundreds and perhaps even thousands of years.

So are we developing this potential for clean energy? The figures say it all. Government funding for the research and development of these energy sources has passed £150 million. Government funding for the research and development of nuclear power has passed £16 *billion*. Labour and Conservative governments have ignored the potential for natural energy and therefore this potential has not been realised. Under the Green Party it would be.

A conservation society

But I keep coming back to the key point we are making. It is not a case of generating as much as possible by whatever means, but of using as little as possible. This is another strand of our conservation society.

Instead of spending our money on generating more energy, we would spend it on insulating homes and workplaces through grants and interest-free loans so that buildings retain their heat and so use far less. This would reduce energy bills, too. We would also strengthen the building regulations so that buildings were made to save heat and not leak it. The amount of fuel and money you can save in this way is astonishing.

Energy Without End features a house built in British Columbia, which has a climate similar to that of southern England. It is four times bigger than the average house in Britain, but it was designed to retain heat. Annual electric heating bill in 1986: £12.

I was on a radio phone-in once when a man came on the line to inform the audience that the Green Party's energy policy would leave people shivering in their own homes. That was the only result he could see from our policy of reducing the use of energy. Like so many, he had been indoctrinated to believe that only more of something could possible solve a problem. I suggested that the reason he heated his home was to keep his family and himself warm. He agreed. An obvious point, but one that had to be made.

What was the difference to him, then, I asked, if he was warm because his home retained the heat that was currently being lost through bad, or no, insulation, and the present situation in which he was warm because although his home leaked heat he could always turn up the dial and burn more energy? 'Well none, I suppose,' he replied. Exactly. The only difference to him would be far smaller fuel bills, but to the Earth and the future the difference between green warmth and grey warmth could be between suicide and survival.

Electrical appliances would have to be made as energy efficient as possible or face financial penalties. The tax system would support energy efficient products and penalise the others. We would introduce a labelling system for all products to show how energy efficient they were: watch the companies change their tune in this area once that was on the way!

A Friends of the Earth report to a House of Lords Committee on Energy showed how with current technology the everyday electrical products we have, like televisions, fridges and the rest, could use between 75 and 90 per cent less energy. What is the best way to eliminate hypothermia which kills many older people in their own homes every winter? To spend the country's money on generating more power at enormous cost and hope the old people will be able to afford it, or to make their homes retain heat so they have to use less and spend less to keep warm?

Everyone benefits from this truly Green approach; people, business and industry cut their fuel costs, and as building insulation is labour intensive, a terrific amount of work will be created all over the country, up to eight times more than you get by spending that same money on generating more energy.

If you add together all the elements of our conservation policies including local production for local need, our national insulation scheme and the end of the throwaway society, we can reduce energy demand in this country by between 55 and 65 per cent over the next fifty years and much of that demand would be met by the clean, natural, energy sources I've mentioned, and others too.

The Green Party would publish an energy index every year setting out how much energy the UK was using and we would aim to reduce the figure by at least one per cent every year as our efficiency policies were phased in. The chances are that we would in practice reduce it by considerably more, once our policies were in full flow and new technology became available.

Our approach will save resources, create far more work, and protect the future for us all. By spending our money in this way we could reduce carbon dioxide emissions from power stations by 50 per cent and at the same time rid the country of nuclear power.

The argument is overwhelming. But look at the British government's response to all this commonsense: they've cut the budget of the Energy Efficiency Office by half.

Nuclear propaganda

Instead, the dangers posed by global warming are being used as the latest justification for nuclear power. I say 'latest' because there have been so many and as each has been discredited so they have thought up new ones.

I have talked already about the consequences for health of nuclear power, but such is the pressure in some circles to expand its use that I should expose the other nuclear propaganda we are asked to believe.

First of all, nuclear power was not introduced to generate energy as such. It was introduced in the fifties as a front for producing plutonium for nuclear weapons. Some of this plutonium went to the Americans for their nuclear weapons, as the authorities have belatedly admitted. We were sold the idea of the peaceful use of the atom when, as the propaganda people of that period have since admitted in television programmes, the idea was to produce weapons grade plutonium and to offset the cost of doing it by generating electricity in the process.

The truths about accidents and radioactive discharges were suppressed so this process could go on unchallenged. Anyone who has the nerve to oppose nuclear power is branded a subversive or unpatriotic, or is accused of trying to undermine the state. Indeed many people around the world who have opposed nuclear power to the point where they were a threat to it, or knew the truth and were planning to make it public, have died in strange circumstances that no one has been able to explain. Big brother is watching very closely when you take on the nuclear power industry and the government and military machine that supports it.

Why doesn't all this happen if you oppose coal-fired or oil-fired energy generation? Because they have not always been closely connected with nuclear weapons production.

In France the democratic process was all but suspended while they pushed through their massive expansion of nuclear power. When the nuclear reprocessing plant at Cap de la Hague was first planned, the local people were told it was going to be a factory to make television sets. As a result, no one opposed it. Later they were told it was going to make washing machines and fridges as well. But slowly, as a three hundred foot chimney began to take shape and a pipe was built leading out to sea, the truth became clear. Even at this point the politicians were still denying what it was. Only when scientists from Marcoule, the first French plutonium production installation, moved in did the authorities admit what was really happening. Other opposition to French nuclear power expansion was more forcibly and brutally dealt with.

The French experience is often given as the example we should follow in the United Kingdom. We are told that France set out to end its dependence on imported oil and that now half the electricity used there comes from nuclear power. Fine. What they don't tell you is that France has reduced its oil imports by relatively little, in fact less than neighbouring countries, because most of the oil is used not to generate electricity, but to power road vehicles.

They also forget to mention that to finance this nuclear power programme, France has taken on a debt of $35 billion and the electricity board, EdF, has said it will never be able to pay back the money it has borrowed. And that their colossal Super-Phénix fast reactor has to be fuelled by five tons of plutonium and it could explode in the same way as a nuclear bomb.

That is not good news for the people of Lyon, just 25 miles away; or Geneva, 31 miles away; or indeed for us in the UK. This monster is much closer to us than Chernobyl and look what effect that had.

If you support this insanity you are seen as patriotic and sensible. If you oppose it you are a subversive who must be dealt with by tear gas and a baton charge. The fact that Super-Phénix produces first class plutonium for the French Force de Frappe nuclear weapons programme has nothing to do with it, of course.

Another justification we have been given for nearly 30 years is that nuclear power is more economic than other forms of energy. In the fifties they said it would be 'too cheap to meter' (the same people told us it was safe) and the books were cooked from then on to hide the truth that it is the most expensive form of energy generation we have ever seen. They did everything they could to mislead us and, supported by successive governments, they made red look black on the balance sheets.

A report for *The Ecologist* called *Nuclear Power – The Real Cost* showed that the cost of building the magnox reactors was at least four times higher than claimed by the Central Electricity Generating Board. The CEGB claimed that the Hinkley Point B reactor was providing cheaper electricity than the Drax A coal-fired station. It was in fact 40 per cent more expensive to build and operate and yet that is the most economic nuclear reactor in the country.

Only more recently after endless independent reports had discredited and ridiculed their figures have the nuclear industry and the government admitted that nuclear power can't be justified on economic grounds.

Then, with their excuses all but dried up, along came the greenhouse effect. They had not wanted to know about it before, but suddenly what a way to justify nuclear power expansion. It's green!

Their claims, as usual, are in conflict with the truth. Nuclear power currently supplies just six per cent of energy used in this country and less than 20 per cent of electricity. To increase that to 50 per cent of electricity would need 24 new nuclear stations in Britain over the next 30 years at a cost at today's prices of £40 billion. When these highly dangerous stations are in place and working, carbon dioxide emissions from Britain's power stations will be reduced by *less than ten per cent*.

That compares with a reduction of 50 per cent through energy conservation and true efficiency without the need for any nuclear power. Which road do you fancy?

To replace coal with nuclear power world-wide would mean building a reactor every day and a half and give all countries the plutonium for nuclear weapons. Even then carbon dioxide emissions would increase from other sources like transport.

If you look at the process in the Green way from start to finish you find that the fossil fuel energy needed to mine the uranium and transport it, produce the cement and transport it, build the reactor, deal with the waste and many other things, will produce an average of 250,000 tonnes of carbon dioxide per reactor per year, according to Nigel Mortimer, an energy analyst at Sheffield Polytechnic.

The authorities also lead us to believe that nuclear power is a limitless source of energy, but in its present form it depends on uranium, the mining of which has destroyed the lands of native peoples like American Indians and Aborigines by releasing radioactivity.

Look at it all in simple terms which is where the truth always awaits us. They want us to accept a process which: contaminates with radioactivity the areas where the uranium is mined; is by far the most expensive form of energy generation; produces lethal waste that no one knows what to do with including plutonium 239 with a half-life of 24,400 years; causes cancer and other diseases; adds daily to the amount of radioactivity in the world which could threaten the very existence of our species if it continues to accumulate; would lay waste a massive area of this crowded country in the event of an accident; has turned the Irish Sea into the most radioactive on Earth; requires reactors that work for around 30 years, take over a hundred years (at least) to dismantle and then must be encased in concrete virtually for ever; and provides an easy and devastating military target for any aggressor.

This is what we are being asked to believe makes good sense. This is what we are asked to believe is good for the environment and the future. This is what is supposed to be 'green'.

The Green Party would cancel all new nuclear power stations immediately, stop the building of any under construction, and phase out all nuclear power in the shortest time possible. Nuclear waste would be stored where we could keep a close watch on it and where we could retrieve it if there was a problem. Apart from that it would be goodbye nuclear power, goodbye to these monuments to our own arrogance and stupidity or at least that of the people we elect to represent us.

Acid rain

There is another environmental hazard lying at the door of energy generation and road traffic which we must also urgently reduce: acid rain.

This was first identified by an English chemist, Robert Angus

Smith, in 1852 when he made the connection between air pollution in industrial Manchester and the acidity of the rain. Well into the 1980s the British government was still denying any such connection and only when they had no arguments left did they have to concede that there may be a problem.

There *is* a problem. Acid rain kills trees, kills lakes, destroys priceless historic buildings and adds hundreds of billions of pounds to the hidden costs of our industrial growth system. Indeed, there may not be enough money to put right the damage that making that money has caused.

More than half the forests of Germany are dead or dying because of air pollution. Forests all over Europe and North America are suffering the same fate, 80 per cent of the lakes and streams in southern Norway are dead or critical, 4,000 lakes in Sweden have no fish life and 20,000 others are unnaturally acidified, and the Acropolis has been eaten away more in the last 30 years than in the previous 2,000!

Hardly surprising when some rainfalls have been found to be as acidic as lemon juice and vinegar – thanks mainly to a combination of sulphur dioxide and oxides of nitrogen produced by burning fossil fuel in power stations, factories and road vehicles.

People are led to believe that the air is cleaner today because we no longer have the smogs we used to have when smoke and fog combined with deadly results. That prompted (the dead body syndrome again) the Clean Air Act of 1956 which created smoke free zones and ended the smogs. It did not, however, end the pollution. Instead of reducing the filth produced by power stations and industry, the act simply moved it away from densely populated areas and built taller chimneys with the idea that it would be dispersed in the atmosphere. It has proved to be a disastrous miscalculation. All it did was travel hundreds of miles, sometimes further, to drop in the rain, snow or fog on someone else's doorstep, or forest, or lake or priceless building.

UK power stations and industry are the biggest producers of

acid rain in Europe with getting on for four million tonnes of sulphur dioxide spewed into the air every year – two thirds of which lands in other countries. More than 600,000 tonnes of sulphur fall on Sweden every year, yet only a sixth of that is produced by Sweden.

Over 40 million tonnes of sulphur are released into the air in Europe every year – that's like taking 66,000 thirty-tonne lorry loads of the stuff and dumping it on the lakes and forests and buildings. No wonder nature can't cope with it, and the evidence is gathering all the time about the threat to human health and food crops which, when you think about it, are obviously going to be affected.

But the UK's record in tackling, or even acknowledging, acid rain is a shocker. We may be the biggest polluters in Western Europe but we still refuse to join the group of countries pledged to reduce acid rain emissions by 30 per cent before 1993. We said the case was 'not proven'. What's more it would cost us money.

Still there is always a judgement day when you mess with nature and ours has arrived. Successive governments (yes, the 'green' tories and socialists) have denied any acid rain damage here. If they acknowledged that, they couldn't go on denying their share of responsibility for what was happening abroad.

What a blow for them, then, with the report in 1987 of a United Nations Survey of acid rain damage in 15 European countries. It found that the UK had more tree damage than anyone else; 67 per cent of conifers had slight to moderate damage and nearly 29 per cent were in the moderate to severe category.

In 1989 the UN issued another report saying that hundreds of millions of trees were sick or dying in the UK because of acid rain. The traditional oak was severely affected.

Acidity builds up over time and how quickly the critical point is reached depends on how much acid rain falls and how naturally acidic the soil is in the first place. One thing's for sure; unless you stop the acid falling that critical point will be reached one day whatever the conditions are. For the UK that time has arrived. Our trees are dying.

Our lakes are going the same way too, and our buildings, like St. Paul's Cathedral, have been badly eaten away by acid air pollution. But never mind, the fortune it costs to repair them will add to growth.

There is also a threat to our water supplies. The acidification of ground water is already causing serious problems in Belgium, Finland, the Netherlands, Norway, Sweden and Germany. There are increased concentrations of dangerous heavy metals in the drinking water because they leach from acid soil, pipes are being corroded, and so are aluminium pots and pans which release aluminium into the food they cook.

The government has been forced, kicking and screaming, to agree to some filters on power station chimneys to de-acidify the emissions, but progress has been painfully and infuriatingly slow. Whenever a situation calls for drastic action they call for further proof that any action is needed.

The Green Party would join the '30 per cent club' immediately and lead Europe to the 75 per cent reduction needed to stop things getting worse. This can be done by chimney filters, investments in new coal-burning technology that can reduce sulphur production by anything up to 90 per cent, and by our conservation policies that will cut enormously the amount of fossil fuels that have to be burned.

The energy policies of the developed world have only been interested in what was good for economic growth and nuclear weapons and not what was necessary to protect the planet. That never entered their minds, for it never enters the minds of those who serve the system.

The time has arrived when we have a choice in theory, but not in practice. We can take the Green option of conservation and true efficiency. That road leads to safety. Or we can take the grey option of more power stations and more waste. That road leads to the edge of the cliff. And over it.

10: On the road to nowhere

Don't it always seem to go
That you don't know what you've got till it's gone?
They pave paradise.
Put up a parking lot.
JONI MITCHELL: *YELLOW TAXI*

There is a beautiful area of north Norfolk that has retained the charm and character lost elsewhere to the unforgiving onslaught of 'progress'.

It is not so much judgement that has protected it, because the great majority of people all around the country are dismayed at what has happened and continues to happen to the character of Britain's rural and urban landscape.

No, the reason so much unspoilt, timeless beauty has survived is that it is tucked up in a corner of East Anglia some way from a major city, and if you pass through it the only place you can end up is the sea. In short, as they say in those parts, it is on the road to nowhere. This has been its saviour because the need to cater for ever increasing traffic travelling longer and longer distances with heavier and heavier loads has not turned its timeless beauty into endless concrete. In so many other places it has. If you are on the road to somewhere you have had it. Our transport system will see to that.

It also sees 248,000 reported accidents a year, more than 5,000 deaths, 70,000 serious injuries and 321,000 casualties in all. More British people have died on the roads since 1945 than died fighting Hitler in the last war.

One significant indication of the lack of environmental under-standing in the grey parties is the way they have always seen the Transport Secretary or opposition spokespeople as second division jobs. It was only in 1981 that transport was given a cabinet rank. Yet the transport issue is crucial to protecting the future. Transport destroys with its roads, its pollution, its sheer weight of numbers, but no one has had the nerve to tackle these problems because they are frightened to death of losing votes. So the madness goes on.

The Green Party would tackle the transport problem in the way it must be tackled if we are to survive. The fantasy must end.

A tale of selfish greed

Road traffic is a massive polluter. The gases and poisons that pour out of exhaust pipes cause cancer and many other diseases, dull the intellect of children, cause acid rain, add significantly to global warming, and waste staggering amounts of irreplaceable resources.

Imagine if someone today brought a new product onto the market which did all those things. There would be clamour for it to be banned. But politicians, even those who see the dangers, dare not take on the car and lorry lobby for fear of their party being banned at the next election.

As a result of this, and lots of 'wink, wink, say no more' at cosy luncheons between civil servants, politicians and the road lobby, we don't have a Department of Transport. We have a Department of Road Building.

The road lobby is headed by the British Road Federation, set up in 1932, and peopled and paid for by the car makers, the lorry companies, oil companies, road builders, concrete and road materials companies and the two motoring organisations, the AA and RAC. Everyone, in fact, who makes money when roads are built.

This public-spirited federation or its constituent parts have opposed: unleaded petrol, catalytic converters which can remove some exhaust pollution, virtually every speed limit, traffic safety schemes which have been shown to save many lives, any restriction on lorries no matter what the effect on people, tachographs which record how long a lorry driver has been at the wheel, compulsory seat belts, and anything that could possibly slow down, tax, or control any motor vehicle in any way, shape or form.

This sorry tale of human greed must put the British Road Federation and its constituent parts among the most selfish, short-sighted, uncaring and irresponsible organisations at large in Britain today. All they are interested in is having more and more roads built and heavier and heavier lorries to run on them. They spend hundreds of thousands of pounds persuading civil servants and politicians to their point of view, although, most of the time, they take very little persuading.

The Federation can afford to be very lavish with its entertainment of such people and with its publicity campaigns because the roads and higher lorry weight limits it has won in this way have made its paymasters billions. How, in the light of this, the Conservative Party can accept donations from some of these companies is quite beyond me. The Liberal-SDP Alliance also accepted money from this source.

The way some Department of Transport officials and politicians have worked to help the Federation against the public interest is best summed up by lorry weight limits.

In the early 1980s a lorry could not weigh fully loaded more than 32 tons. The Federation wanted 44 tons, but the Conservative government came under terrific pressure from the public and environmentalists and decided on 40 tons. Still the pressure continued and they were forced in the end to reduce it further to 38 tons.

Then came the Department's little wheeze. Without agreement by parliament, they changed the rules so that a lorry had to be five per cent over the limit before police could order the driver to remove some of the load, and ten per cent over the limit before the driver could be prosecuted. What did that make the weight a lorry could carry before the driver was liable to prosecution? 41.8 tons. And 20 per cent of the lorries checked are over even that limit.

We now have the prospect of lorries weighing 40 tons (plus ten per cent) which will demand a hundred million pound investment in bridge strengthening alone. One haulage spokesman said he looked forward to the day when 50 ton lorries can travel legally from Turkey to Scotland.

They say bigger lorries means fewer lorries, i.e. juggernauts are good for the environment. Then how come more lorries were on the road after the weight increases than before?

The true cost of lorries

Even at 38 tons a lorry does more damage than 100,000 cars and that's a conservative estimate – some say it is 200,000. This is just one way we are subsidising the road haulage industry, the road building giants and centralised production by major companies. We are paying for their colossal profits with our taxes, not only in road building and repairs and environmental decline, but in countless other ways like the cost of accidents caused by heavy lorries, the cost of medical treatment, police and damage to buildings.

They also fracture water mains, gas mains and sewers. Most of the annual water repair budget is spent on damage caused by lorries, and gas explosions have been traced to fractured mains, again caused by the same culprit.

We must add all that to the cost of centralised production and all the things we buy, including food, before we an arrive at the true price we are paying for them. The indirect, hidden costs are tremendous and make the system ludicrously inefficient. So remember the next time you shop at Tesco or Asda or the other major supermarkets that the price you see on the labels is only part of what you are actually paying for what you buy.

But the road building goes on and on 'to meet the needs of industry' and more roads are followed by more traffic. You can turn an unopened road into a traffic jam by putting the scissors to the tape.

The M25, the ring road around London, was going to ease the capital's traffic problems when it was opened by Margaret Thatcher. In no time it was a permanent jam in the rush hour and what was the Government's answer to it? To add another lane!

A traffic policeman was asked by the BBC's Panorama programme what would happen if the M25 was expanded to four lanes:

'You'll have a four-lane parking lot,' he said.

'Five lanes?'

'A five-lane parking lot.'

'Six lanes?'

'Just the same.'

Then what? Add another and another and another? Where does it end? It is a nonsense. The history of roads is that the traffic will expand to fit them. New roads just encourage people to drive until the new roads are clogged and then they build more new roads. Most importantly, this policy encourages the very pollution that is threatening the future.

Cutting the traffic

It is not more roads we want, but fewer vehicles. I doubt, however, that such an obvious conclusion would ever get through to a succession of road-building transport ministers like Ernest Marples, whose company helped to build the M4 which he had sanctioned. It was Mr. Marples, gleefully supported by the British Road Federation, who appointed Dr. Beeching to decimate our railway system, a policy continued by the Labour government that followed him.

I doubt, also, if people like Nicholas Ridley would ever see the sense of the Green approach. When he was Transport Secretary he was against wheel clamps and even one-way streets because he said they interfered with the democratic rights of motorists. The same, then, must apply in his view to zebra crossings, traffic policemen, school crossing wardens and traffic lights. Indeed, that appears to be the case. He wanted to remove 30 per cent of London's traffic lights to increase the liberty of drivers.

This was Mr. Ridley's assessment of the traffic problem:

> The private motorist . . . wants the chance to live a life that
> gives him a new dimension of freedom – freedom to go where
> he wants, when he wants, and for as long as he wants.

Try telling that to the rush hour motorists on the M25 or on any other road in and out of London and the other cities. Try telling that to bank-holiday drivers. Or to the people who live a life of hell and ill health alongside the roads that bring this 'freedom'.

About half the lung disease in the United States is caused by air pollution and cases of cancer are 12 per cent higher in traffic congested cities than elsewhere. The densely populated UK must be as bad or worse. The US are now looking at air quality standards that can only be met by reduced traffic levels and improved public transport, along with more cycling and walking, the most non-polluting transport of all.

We should not forget that far more people don't have cars than do – mostly the less well off, for obvious reasons. What about their freedom? They are free to be poisoned, to be imprisoned by cut-backs in public transport in favour of road building, to see their communities cut in two or replaced by urban motorways or interchanges, to live with the constant traffic jams, the fumes, the noise, the dangers for them and their children.

What about the freedom of people not to see the forests die from acid rain or the climate change with global warming? Such considerations do not go on the system's balance sheet. That's why we are up the creek.

The story of UK transport policy, as Mick Hamer explains so well in *Wheels Within Wheels*, is of weak or compliant ministers and civil servants supporting or caving in to the road lobby, road enquiries rigged to stifle opposition, and a progressive dismantling of public transport. Time and time again governments have fought to stop things like unleaded petrol and catalytic converters until they could resist no more.

I can remember few more despairing moments than picking up the paper after months of stories about traffic chaos and how Britain was coming to a standstill, and seeing the government's response. A twelve billion pound road building plan. Commonsense and sanity are long overdue. The polluters must pay the full cost of what they do and it must become more economic to protect than destroy.

We would phase out road tax as we know it today and recover that revenue from an increase in fuel tax. This way those who drive the most miles, use the most finite resources and create the most pollution, would pay the most money. Those who need a car for essential transport, say in rural areas, but don't travel that far that often, would pay much less.

This would immediately make people think about the way they use their cars, about the fuel economy of the car and whether a small one would be better, and it would make the manufacturers approach fuel economy in a much more radical way than they have so far. Fuel-saving cars would be the best sellers.

We would insist on catalytic converters, naturally, but we should not believe that is enough. Converters neutralise some of the pollution, but have no effect on carbon dioxide emissions;

indeed they may even increase them. It will also be a long, long time before every car has a catalytic converter under the present system.

There would be no increase overall in the amount of land used for car parks. That would include out of town shopping centres which demand that people use their cars. We would discourage them in other ways, too.

Only those roads that could be shown to have significant environmental benefits would be built and apart from those and road repairs, spending on roads would cease. There is simply no point in going on building more roads, taking more country-side or pulling down more buildings, disrupting more communi-ties, and spending endless amounts of money just to create even bigger traffic jams.

We often forget the other hidden costs of road building: the beautiful areas that are despoiled by the extraction of road materials, and how the arrival of a new roads opens up land for further development. How many times have we seen a new road across previously inaccessible land followed by building development? The rainforests could not be destroyed at the present rate if roads had not been built into them.

The Green Party would shift that road-building money on to public transport, which is greatly more efficient. A full bus is a moving traffic jam because if everyone on board was in a car a jam there would be. If everyone on a full train travelled by car there would a major snarl up. In London, buses are just one per cent of the vehicles on the roads, but carry 30 per cent of people travelling by road.

I remember standing on Leicester station one day when a goods train came speeding through. I lost count of the number of wagons, but it was past and gone in a few seconds. Had they been lorries, Leicester would have taken all day to recover from the disruption.

The increase in fuel prices and the switch of investment from road to rail would ensure that goods would be cheaper taken by rail than by juggernaut. This would reflect the reality that when you add on the hidden costs of road freight it is a great deal more expensive now than rail. We would bring that fact on to the balance sheet.

Only much smaller lorries and vans would be needed to take goods from the rail head to the customer and we would phase in a *decrease* in permitted lorry sizes and weights over a period of years. (I think the leader of the British Road Federation has just fainted. When he comes round, tell him there will also be speed limiters on bigger vehicles so they could not break the speed limit and those limits will be lower anyway to save lives and resources currently being wasted by excessive speed.)

We would expand the rail and bus network, including rural and cross country routes, and improve frequency, capacity and relative costs. There would be trams, light railways or underground trains to replace car use in the cities. More control over transport policy and the money to achieve it would be given to local councils to devise schemes that best suit their areas.

Planning regulations would be changed and incentives given for companies that need to distribute long distance to locate alongside railway lines so they can link directly with the rail network. At the moment they locate near motorway interchanges to link directly with the juggernaut network.

Towns for people

The Green Party believes that towns and cities and everywhere else should be run for people, not road vehicles, and our policies would do that. There is a myth that Green politics has nothing to offer urban areas. This is so wrong.

Most Green Party members I know live in urban areas – and nowhere needs greening more urgently than our neglected and abused inner cities and built-up areas where 80 per cent of us live. At the heart of that is putting people before the internal combustion engine.

The speed limits in residential streets would be reduced to below 20 miles an hour to make them safer for everyone, especially children. A West German government study showed that this could reduce road deaths by half. A child in the UK is twice as likely to die on the roads as a child in the Netherlands and three times as likely as one in Sweden because our traffic restraint policies are so poor or non-existent. The British Road Federation or its members fight every attempt to improve them.

We would introduce speed humps – sleeping policemen – to all residential streets and there would be other measures to ensure that speeds were restricted. There would be many more car-free areas and priority would be given to the needs of pedestrians and cyclists.

I always find it incredible that someone who cycles, producing no pollution and keeping themselves fit and healthy, is seen by some as a bit weird and extreme, when someone who sits in a traffic jam for hours ever day spewing out acid rain and other unpleasant rubbish from the exhaust pipe and getting home or to work all wound up from sheer frustration, is somehow seen as sensible and credible. My goodness, our values have gone haywire.

Our determination to make cities for people and not for cars also includes urban nature reserves and farms, and creating community councils to give people a say in what happens in their area. We must re-build our urban communities which have been ravaged by our obsession with the motor vehicle and the re-development that has made way for it.

Moving most of our journeys from road to rail and other public transport is essential, but that's only part of it. What we really have to do is reduce the need for motorised transport. Our policy of local production for local needs would do that in a very big way, but we must also stop putting houses in one area and work in another, so creating a sizeable journey twice a day for large numbers of people. We must integrate housing and work much more whenever we have the opportunity, and that can be done as big polluting factories are replaced by cleaner, smaller scale businesses.

We have to discourage the out of town shopping complexes and put shops where people are. Unless we turn back from the course charted by our governments, particularly since the war, we are heading for big trouble.

Just look at what our vehicles, mainly heavy lorries, release into the atmosphere every year: 228,000 tons of carbon monoxide, 167,000 of nitrous oxide, 37,000 of hydrocarbons, 37,000 of sulphur dioxide, 35,000 of particulates, plus all the carbon dioxide.

We think that's bad enough on top of the other costs and consequences of road transport, but we haven't seen anything yet. Official forecasts suggest that the volume of traffic will increase by between 83 and 142 per cent by 2025.

Does anyone really believe we can go on like this? It is not only that beautiful corner of Norfolk that is on the road to nowhere. So is Britain's transport system – and it is taking us with it.

11:   Peacemakers – and proud of it

The unleashed power of the atom has changed everything except our way of thinking ... We need an essentially new way of thinking if mankind is to survive.
ALBERT EINSTEIN

We no longer have a choice between violence or non-violence. The choice is between non-violence and non existence.
MARTIN LUTHER KING

If you put a gun to your head and say 'Touch me and I'll shoot', you would be giving a perfect impression of the NATO 'defence' policy.

It is called flexible response: attack us with conventional weapons and we'll destroy the whole of Europe (including our bit) with nuclear ones. Very flexible.

They sell us this under the theory known appropriately as MAD, Mutually Assured Destruction. The theory is that no one will use nuclear weapons because they know that nuclear weapons would be used against them in return. This is the way the nuclear 'deterrent' has been sold so successfully to the British people.

The Labour Party and the Liberal Democrats have both caved in under pressure instead of arguing their case, and both have committed themselves to keeping even Britain's independent nuclear weapons. The Green Party will not cave in. Why should we exchange sanity for insanity, commonsense for no sense?

We would dismantle all nuclear weapons on UK soil in the shortest time possible, close all United States bases in this country, and begin a phased withdrawal from NATO. We will justify all three decisions with enormous confidence because what is happening today is simply not credible.

Let us take each one in turn, starting with nuclear weapons.

The lunacy of nuclear defence

While governments and the military are selling us the nuclear deterrent theory, they don't tell us that part of NATO's policy is to use nuclear weapons even *before* the Soviet Union use theirs, and I offer you one stunning example of the lunacy the Green Party would free us from.

The details of a NATO exercise to rehearse the actual conduct of a war were leaked to the German magazine, *Der Spiegel*. The exercise put into practice the 'general political guidelines' for the use of nuclear weapons decided by NATO's Planning Group.

The story was reported by *The Observer* in the spring of 1989:

[The guidelines meant that] instead of a 'warning shot' being fired at the Soviet Union when its conventional forces had broken through Western defences, the Americans called for a substantial nuclear strike on Eastern European Targets: 21 warheads or bombs, each of 100 kilotons (the Hiroshima Bomb was of 13 kilotons).

The man playing the German Chancellor in the government bunker in the Ahr Valley near Bonn, Waldemar Schreckenberger, broke with normal practice and called the real Chancellor for advice. The Europeans managed to get the number of atomic bombs in the strike reduced from 21 to 17.

Only one bomb was dropped on the Soviet Union itself, and that did not come from the Americans, but from a British Tornado stationed in West Germany. The conclusion in Bonn was that Washington wanted to avoid provoking Moscow into a retaliatory strike on the United States.

Three warheads fell on East Germany, but taking West

German sensibilities into account NATO Command ordered other allies to fire them.

According to reports *Der Spiegel* obtained, the scenario then departed from any reality. The Soviet Union did not (according to the NATO theory) respond with nuclear weapons, but continued its conventional push and the NATO Supreme Commander, General John Galvin, called for a second nuclear strike.

Two warheads were destined for West Germany and two for Turkey, to destroy invading troops. Both Bonn and Ankara protested, but to no avail.

Schreckenberger called the real Chancellor again and was told: 'Stop this idiocy.' West Germany pulled out of the exercise three days early.

The main point of the criticism is that the American perception of 'flexible response' allows for the destruction of Europe, including both Germanys.

So there you have our nuclear defence policy. If we are attacked with conventional weapons we unleash enough fire-power to destroy Europe, but there will be no nuclear response from the Soviet Union who will just carry on with their tank attack as if nothing had happened.

I ask you.

NATO: the unequal alliance

NATO is an organisation run by America for America to ensure that any war involving America takes place in Europe and not America. Did you know the top two command posts, Supreme Allied Commander Europe and Supreme Allied Commander Atlantic are *always* held by Americans? Why, if this really is an alliance of equals? But, of course, it isn't. Apart from the British and French weapons, all nuclear warheads in Western Europe are owned by America and the US President could order their use without even consulting other countries.

People have become so used to having nuclear weapons around that they have forgotten what we are dealing with here. One nuclear missile can carry as much explosive power as that expended in the whole of the Second World War. The Hiroshima bomb, as I've said, was of 13 kilotons. One missile today can be of 6,000 kilotons.

Remember the damage done across Europe by the radiation released by the Chernobyl explosion? That was one tenth of a kiloton! When you see how much radiation would be released by nuclear weapons, what can you say about people who sanction their use as part of a NATO 'defence' strategy? Who's crazy, us or them?

No one with an ounce of sense would even contemplate using them because both attacker and attacked would reap the consequences, one from the explosion and the other from the radioactive fall-out that would make large areas of the world unable to sustain life. Even a limited nuclear attack would bring the 'nuclear winter', as soot and dust from the explosions and fires gathered in the atmosphere to block out the light and warmth of the sun. Both sides would suffer in this artificial 'ice age', especially from catastrophic crop failure.

The entire nuclear deterrent argument is based on the belief that although there are many tens of thousands of these weapons of mass destruction, not one of them will ever be released by accident, mistake or for any other reason in the whole of the rest of time. Do you really believe that? The nuclear deterrence theory cannot afford to fail. Not once. Not ever. Or else.

The state of the art technology that controls our defence gives constant false alarms of imminent nuclear attack because it is far from foolproof. It was state of the art electronics that could not tell the difference between an Iranian airliner and a military jet. This led to an airliner full of innocent people being blown from the sky. There was much criticism, obviously, of the American naval officer who gave the order to shoot, but think of the pressure he was under not knowing if his ship was about to be attacked. We do silly things sometimes under enormous pressure and what more pressure is there than having a finger on the nuclear button? The biggest threat of nuclear devastation is not from war, but from an accident or mistake.

This is made worse by technological 'advances' that have improved the speed and accuracy of nuclear weapons to the point that to retaliate against an attack you will have to press the button when you *think* an attack is imminent. Any later and your own missiles could be taken out in large numbers before they could be released. At times of tension, even imaginary tension, the itchy finger on the button will become even itchier.

If anyone still believes after what I've said that our nuclear weapons are always in the hands of competent people then why are there around 50 nuclear weapons on the bottom of the oceans where they have 'slipped off' ships or gone down in submarine accidents? The person or technology hasn't been born or invented that doesn't make mistakes.

Why have we come so close to disaster in this country when planes carrying nuclear weapons have only avoided crashing by the grace of God? The government and military say these bombs could not cause a nuclear explosion – though there are some who dispute this – but the authorities do admit that the conventional explosive around a warhead can, and would, scatter radiation over a wide area of several miles.

Yet the government machines, ours as much as any, have so indoctrinated people with propaganda and misinformation that opinion polls have consistently gone against non-nuclear defence; the possession of weapons of mass destruction has been seen as sane, while anyone who wants to get rid of them is seen as somehow unpatriotic and a threat to the state. That's terribly sad because it is so terribly wrong.

How can women who are so committed to peace and nuclear disarmament that they spend their days and nights at Greenham Common be treated with such ridicule and abuse? They have got more guts and commitment than those who ridicule them could begin to comprehend.

'No help, no hope'

Earl Mountbatten of Burma would certainly understand why we are so opposed to the nuclear illusion. He was a Commander-in-Chief of sea and land in the Second World War, and hardly a man you would call a pacifist.

Yet he said in a famous speech back in 1979 that he had never found the arguments for nuclear defence convincing, especially when we had missiles a 'thousand times more dreadful' than those that dropped on Japan.

He went on:

A new war can hardly fail to involve the all-out use of nuclear weapons. Such a war would not drag on for years. It could be all over in a matter of days.

And when it was all over what would the world be like? Our fine great buildings, our homes will exist no more. The thousands of years it took to develop our civilisation will have been in vain. Our works of art will be lost. Radio, television, newspapers, will disappear. There will be no means of transport. There will be no hospitals. No help can be expected for a few mutilated survivors in any town to be sent from a neighbouring town – there will be no neighbouring towns left, no neighbours, there will be no help, there will be no hope.

As a military man who has been given half a century of active service I say in all sincerity that the nuclear arms race has no military purpose. Wars cannot be fought with nuclear weapons. Their existence only adds to our perils because of the illusions which they have generated.

There are powerful voices around the world who still give credence to the old Roman precept – if you desire peace, prepare for war. This is absolute nuclear nonsense and I repeat – it is a disastrous misconception to believe that by increasing the total uncertainty one increases one's own certainty.

> After all, it is true that science offers us almost unlimited opportunities, but it is up to us, the people, to make the moral and philosophical choices and since the threat to humanity is the work of human beings, it is up to man to save himself from himself.

Absolutely right.

The Labour Party may find it embarrassing to be asked 'Would you press the button?', but the Green Party has no such problem. Would we press the button? Would we destroy Europe? No, no, no, never, never, never, and soon after we came to office there would be no button to press.

The Green Party could never be anything but non-nuclear. You can't stand for the protection of the future and then support the possession of weapons that would destroy it in a day.

Ending the delusion of grandeur

But there are other reasons, too. We want our nuclear disarmament in the UK to stimulate multilateral agreements between NATO and the Warsaw Pact until all nuclear weapons are gone. The Soviet Union has suggested this already, but the West has not wanted to know. If NATO lost the nuclear weapons based in Britain, they would be forced to address these proposals with more commitment, especially as other NATO countries, like West Germany, are getting increasingly jumpy about being no more than America's first line of defence.

It shows how uncommitted the UK has been to nuclear disarmament that we still have our own nuclear weapons at immense cost at a time when Europe is full of the things. What is even more hard to take is that all the other parties are now committed to Trident.

Why are we the only full member of NATO that considers it necessary to have our own nuclear weapons, especially when they probably can't be used without American back-up? It has nothing to do with defence and everything to do with political status. It allows us the delusion that we are still a great world power when all we are doing is dancing to America's tune.

We would start a phased withdrawal from NATO because it is a block to disarmament. It is so unwieldy and bureaucratic that even its own officials describe it as an oil-tanker: hard to slow down and almost impossible to change course.

The power of those in control comes from the 'Soviet Threat'. It is this which is used to justify more weapons, more resources, more money, and so more power for those in charge. It is an empire builder's dream. So, not surprisingly, the weapons reductions so far have been made not because of NATO but President Gorbachev, who is desperate to disarm because the Soviet Union can no longer afford to go on with its military expenditure at past levels.

Even then, much of the reduction is cosmetic. We agree to take away some weapons, but then 'modernise' what we have left and increase their destructive capacity. Trident is the great example of this. With Trident replacing Polaris as the British nuclear weapon our destructive capacity increases many times and yet we are supposed to be involved in disarmament!

NATO doesn't want total nuclear disarmament because its power is diminished. Every arms control agreement has to be forced upon it by President Gorbachev's initiatives and by European public opinion, which no longer buys the line about a Soviet invasion. If we announced our intention to pull out, along with the removal of nuclear weapons and US bases, NATO's complacency would suffer such a shock that it would have to join the real world and start negotiating seriously for the elimination of all nuclear weapons on both sides.

NATO is also a power bloc with a few at the centre having enormous power over the lives of everyone in Western Europe. We are committed to dismantling such power structures, not being part of them. Nor, surely, is it right that the defence of

Europe should be run at all times on the basis of what is right for America. Yet that is how NATO is run.

All US bases and facilities (over 150 of them) would be closed because we are supposed to be an independent country, not an American aircraft carrier. If anyone thinks that the UK is not an occupied country they should watch what happens when the Americans are asked to go. After all, American intelligence knew what was happening in New Zealand when the Rainbow Warrior was bombed, but they didn't tell the New Zealand government because it had refused to allow US ships carrying nuclear weapons into New Zealand ports. It didn't matter that a foreign power, France, was planning to bomb a Greenpeace ship full of innocent people. The New Zealanders had not done as America wanted, so they had to be taught a lesson.

What do you think they would try to do to the Green Party if we got close to government, or if our arguments in opposition were making people question the American role in the UK? I dread to think; we will not be bowed, whatever the pressure, though there will be a great deal of unseen activity to ensure that we are never elected or that we don't win over the British people to our view. This would take the form of undermining the party and individuals within it in a variety of ways. As we continue to progress, you watch and see. We are taking on people in many areas with fantastic personal and economic power. They are not going to give that up easily.

Making the Green peace

We have not had peace in the world since the last war. There have been more wars than ever before. We have not had peace in Europe since the last war. We have had an armed truce, a balance of terror. That may be many things, but peace it is not.

If you want real peace that will reduce tension and fear to a minimum then you don't arm everybody with enough weapons to kill every man, woman and child on the planet twelve times over. Instead, you ensure that while everyone can defend themselves vigorously and effectively, they don't have the ability to attack others. That's how the Green Party defence policy works. It is truly defensive.

Goodness knows how many nuclear weapons are aimed at Britain, because we have goodness knows how many aimed at the Warsaw Pact. We fear them, at least we are encouraged to, and they fear us, or at least they are encouraged to.

Uniting one people by the fear and hatred of another is an old political trick. Hitler did it with the Jewish people, for instance, and it is going on constantly all over the world. It has been useful for both American and Soviet governments to promote the 'threat'. The Green Party offers another way.

We would possess only conventional weapons exclusively suited to defending ourselves. It is a military fact that you don't need parity in weapons with an aggressor to repel an invasion. Defending your own country can be done with considerably fewer resources than you need to attack another. To deter an aggressor you don't need the means to turn Europe into a wasteland; you need to show a potential enemy that attacking you would mean dire consequences for them and no gain at the end of it.

A Green Britain would have the latest surveillance systems, and expand research and development into better ones, as well as into anti-tank and anti-aircraft weapons, mines and a highly efficient system of sabotage and non co-operation that would make it impossible for a foreign power to control this country.

When you think that the Soviet Union had control of Afghanistan's capital and yet they couldn't occupy the country because of a resistance movement that, in effect, made it up as it went along, what chance has anyone got of occupying Britain? Imagine you are thinking of doing it. First of all, why are you doing it? What are you hoping to gain when, if you are the Soviet Union, you are having terrible trouble with your own economy and your own regional disputes? More of the same somewhere else is the last thing you need.

If you can answer that, you know that attacking what would be a neutral country that has no offensive capability would mean there would be a substantial political, diplomatic and economic price to pay in your relationships with other countries.

You know that you will be faced with the very latest defensive systems that would be extremely difficult and costly to penetrate.

You know that should you get through, a large section of the civilian population could be mobilised very quickly to make life hell for you should you actually land.

You know that Britain would be a country where most government decisions were made in local regions and communities and running the show from a central point would be near impossible.

You know that a highly organised system of sabotage would take out all the key roads, bridges, railways, runways, and communications equipment if you looked like breaking through.

You know that there would be a pre-arranged plan of resistance by highly trained people in every region that would mean you would have to be on constant alert every minute you were in the country.

You know that there would be no co-operation from the mass of the population who would know how to take out key equipment in the areas in which they work.

Still fancy attacking?

Gandhi knew the truth of all this fifty years ago when he said: 'One hundred thousand Englishmen simply cannot control 350 million Indians if those Indians refuse to co-operate.' And, of course, they couldn't. The Englishmen had to leave.

It is not nuclear weapons or enormous 'defence' spending that is changing the face of Eastern Europe, but mass protest and non-co-operation: *people power*. The same phenomenon will eventually defeat the evil of apartheid in South Africa. Non-violent resistance is far more powerful in forcing change than the bomb or the gun.

It is said that we would be open to nuclear attack if we didn't have nuclear weapons, but remember those figures again. The Chernobyl explosion was one tenth of a kiloton. One missile can involve 6,000 kilotons. We would get the blast, they would get the radiation and both of us would get the nuclear winter. Again, I ask, why would they want to inflict that on themselves?

Increasing numbers of people now accept that the Soviet Union has no intention of attacking us, but, they ask, what if Libya or Iran get the bomb?

Well, how can we stop them if we have it? If other countries are saying they need nuclear weapons as a deterrent, then Libya can say it has been attacked by America from British bases and it needs nuclear weapons to stop a repeat. Iran can say it was attacked by Iraq and it needs the bomb to deter a repeat. How can we argue with that if we are saying the same? But would it be a good thing if they had the bomb? Hardly.

The argument that we should have nuclear weapons means that, if you take it to its logical conclusion, every country in the world should have them to deter attack. How ridiculous.

The only safe nuclear weapons are dismantled nuclear weapons. With Mr. Gorbachev in the Kremlin and with the Soviet Union so desperate to cut arms spending, we now have the opportunity to do that. Once they are gone, the United Nations should set up an organisation to ensure that no one possesses nuclear weapons or is in the process of making them. Failure to permit UN inspections should result in immediate and total economic sanctions by all member countries until those inspections have been allowed. The same should apply to chemical and biological weapons.

A non-nuclear, non-aggressive defence policy is not a Green utopia. It is already happening in countries like Sweden. Are they occupied? Are they at war? They haven't seen fighting for

170 years. And are they governed by the far left? You must be joking.

The Green Party would campaign to replace NATO with a much looser alliance of non-nuclear European countries who based their defence on just that: *defence*. Each country would have its own independent arrangements, but everyone would come to each other's aid if attacked.

As long as they meet the 'only defence' criteria, we would want to see Eastern European countries in this alliance as well so we can break up the power blocs and the hyped-up hostility between them. We also want to see the European Community replaced by a Europe of regions in which the present Eastern bloc regions are a part. Given what we have seen in Eastern Europe, anything becomes possible.

We are not saying this can happen tomorrow, but it is something we must aim towards. Things can move very quickly once the ability to attack each other is removed. Who wants to spend resources they can't afford on maintaining a buffer zone when there is nothing to threaten you?

We must end this belief that you must always dominate and threaten to get what you want. Let's start shaking hands, not fists.

Trading in death

Our obsession with more and more weapons is causing death and destruction all over the world. We sell weapons to other countries to win influence for economic reasons – and because it reduces the unit cost of the weapons we use ourselves. The pursuit of these longer production runs has powered the arms trade. As Mrs. Thatcher said at a Farnborough International Air Show dinner: 'The prospects for overseas orders will be a factor which will play an increasing part in deciding our own operational requirement.'

The United Kingdom is now one of the world's biggest arms

suppliers through an organisation paid for by the taxpayer called the Defence Sales Organisation. It puts on the big arms sale shows like the British Army Equipment Exhibition at Aldershot. We will sell to anyone who wants to buy. Of the 94 countries invited to one Aldershot exhibition, 43 were listed by Amnesty International for abusing human rights.

We have the nerve to say we stand up for human rights while at the same time supplying arms to despots and dictators. They are used to prop up dreadful regimes and to suppress the legitimate demands of people for democracy and decent treatment. We supplied arms to China: when arms were used to slaughter innocent people we announced we would stop the sales. A lot of good that was to the students, wasn't it?

Since 1945 arms sold in increasing numbers to less developed countries have been used in wars and conflicts that have cost 25 million lives. France is supposed to be an ally of Britain in the defence of Europe, yet who supplied Argentina with the Exocet missiles that did so much damage in the Falklands? France.

It has nothing to do with what's right or wrong. Money and economic influence are the ruling criteria. The Green Party would end all sales of arms from the UK, except for defensive systems to neutral countries. The production and sale of leg irons and torture equipment now being freely sold abroad by British companies would also end immediately and those firms not required to make our truly defensive weapons would be converted to peaceful production for the needs of people.

It is a myth that arms spending is an effective way to create jobs. As weapons technology is becoming more and more sophisticated, so it is becoming less and less labour intensive. The money spent on arms may be soaring, but the number of people employed is declining. We can create more useful work for the same or less money if we switch skills and infrastructure from arms to needs. As one Lucas Aerospace worker said:

The government, that is me the taxpayer, buys Harrier jump jets and medical equipment like kidney machines. Lucas say it's profitable to produce Harriers, but not profitable to produce kidney machines. People are dying because there aren't enough kidney machines to go round. We collected pennies on street corners and in pubs to buy a kidney machine for a little boy who was dying because the National Health Service couldn't provide one. The money was raised in no time. I wonder if somehow things were reversed and it became profitable to produce kidney machines and unprofitable to produce aircraft, how many people would give pennies to government ministers or civil servants on street corners when they wanted a new Harrier or Tornado.

It is more profitable for companies to produce arms because they can't lose. The government guarantees them costs, plus an agreed profit, which is hardly a spur to be efficient for a start.

The jobs myth

More than 50 per cent of Britain's publicly-funded research goes on arms development. Organisations like the Medical Research Council get only a fraction of that. Just think what you could do with those sort of resources to find the answers we really need to progress without harming the planet. Just think of the useful work that money could create and the good things it could do. The United States Bureau of Labor Statistics has revealed that one billion dollars spent on arms creates 75,710 jobs; on transport, 92,071; on health care, 138,939; on education 187,299.

The Transport and General Workers Union published a first class booklet called *A Better Future For Defence Jobs*, which showed how much better it would be to convert arms production to the alternatives and how it can and has been done. We could keep arms workers on full pay during the conversion period and still be much better off than paying them to produce arms, such are the massive costs involved in arms production!

The real enemy

The saddest thing about the arms tragedy – and tragedy is the word – is that we have identified the wrong enemy. The enemy of the West is not the Soviet Union, nor are we their enemy. The real enemy of the West is ourselves and the economic monster we have created, the dragon that is destroying us and the future.

To tackle and control that we have to stop wasting resources on arms in this stupid, irresponsible way. The military machine consumes five per cent of the world's oil production and more aluminium, copper, nickel and platinum are used by the military than for all purposes in Africa, Asia, and Latin America put together. I reckon that when the last tree has been cut down, the last water supply poisoned and the last land degraded, there will still be someone with a pair of field glasses in the West saying 'I wonder when the Russians are coming?' And there will be someone in the East looking through another pair of field glasses saying 'I wonder when NATO will attack?'

It's so sad, it really is.

The threat of war comes from the very policies we are pursuing at the expense of the planet. The threat does not come from the Soviet Union or anyone else invading the United Kingdom or Western Europe. It comes from continued environmental degradation. War will come when the rich countries have degraded their own land so it cannot provide for them or when the depletion of natural resources means there are not enough to go round. This is when today's major powers, in the death throes of the system, will fight over who has what of the land and resources that are left. That is the real threat of nuclear war and to avoid it we must avoid the circumstances that will trigger it. That means spending less on arms and more on people and the planet. It's the opposite of today's perceived wisdom.

How can it be that we have got our priorities so wrong? How can it be that the money needed to give everyone in the world enough to eat, an adequate home, adequate education and adequate health care for a year is spent on arms every two weeks?

How can it be that the cost of one missile is more than the combined annual income of 10,000 people in a poor country?

How can it be that the United States can spend half a billion pounds on *one* aircraft when there is so much misery which that money could relieve?

How can it be that the cost of one nuclear submarine is more than the money spent in a year on the education of 160 million children in poor countries?

How can it be that this world spends on arms two million dollars a minute while a child dies from preventable disease every two seconds. How can it be?

These are the real questions that should be posed to the politicians and military men who waste the Earth's riches to produce weapons that will destroy it. World military expenditure has passed a trillion dollars a year and more scientists are working on weapons research than any other subject. We say that is an outrage. Who's crazy, us or them?

The arms story shows so clearly how humankind have lost their way, lost their grip on reality. This can't go on or we won't go on. We have to stop squaring up to each other and start co-operating in a new sense of partnership. We must join together to fight the real battle to win back the future.

To do that, we need total nuclear disarmament and serious conventional disarmament until we have only weapons of defence. That's the way to true peace and true friendship because you can't shake hands with a clenched fist.

12: Dying to be cured

'Twas a dangerous cliff, as they freely confessed,
Though to walk near its crest was so pleasant:
But over its terrible edge there had slipped,
A duke and many a peasant;
So the people said something would have to be done,
But their projects did not all tally:
Some said, 'Put a fence round the edge of the cliff';
Some 'An ambulance down in the valley.'

Then an old man remarked, 'It's a marvel to me,
That people give far more attention,
To repairing results than to stopping the cause,
When they'd much better aim at prevention;
Let us stop at its source all this mischief' cried he,
'Come neighbours and friends, let us rally;
If the cliff we will fence, we might almost dispense,
With the ambulance down in the valley.'
JOSEPH MALINES

The system measures everything in throughput. Even health. Challenge prime ministers about the problems of the health service and they will retort: 'We are treating more patients than ever before.'

The Green Party's response to that is: Why?

Why are we treating more patients than ever before? Why are so many people ill? Treating more patients than at any time in history doesn't measure success, but failure on a colossal scale. The aim of any health policy should be to stop people getting ill, but ours is primarily interested in trying to cure them once the damage is done. Yet again it is the fire brigade approach. Yet again they fail to see the connections between cause and effect.

Britain's national health policy is like the policeman who was so busy trying to pull people out of the river that he didn't have the time to go upstream and arrest the guy who was pushing them in. The truth is that if we poison and pollute the air we breathe, the water we drink and the food we eat, our health is going to suffer. If we are given powerful drugs we don't need, our health will suffer. If we have a system that creates enormous stress for both winners and losers, our health will suffer. If we smoke, drink too much, eat too much, and abuse our bodies through ignorance or complacency, our health will suffer.

How the NHS has lost its way

These are the things we must tackle if we are to stop the National Health Service coming apart at the seams before very long. People can argue about whether it should have more money or use what it has more wisely. What we surely can no longer argue about is that we can't go on indefinitely chasing ever decreasing demand with ever increasing resources. Once more we are heading for disaster unless we radically change our approach.

The NHS is a wonderful concept, but it has lost its way. When it was set up after the war, the theory was that giving the population access to free health care at the point of need would mean a healthier nation. This, so the theory went, would mean that over time fewer people would need treatment and the health service would need fewer resources. The reality is somewhat different: the concentration of effort on curing and not preventing has created a spiral in which an increasingly unhealthy nation is chasing more and more resources. The time must come when ill health will outstrip the country's ability to pay for it. Indeed we are approaching that time very rapidly.

We are told that the money we spend on modern medicine

has increased life expectancy dramatically and made us all much more healthy. It's not wholly true. The biggest leaps in life expectancy and health have been the result of social reformers, not medicine. It was the improvements in things like housing, sewers and water supplies that had the major impact on health, not modern medical techniques. More money has been spent on medicine and research in the last 20 years than in the whole of previous history, but we have comparatively little to show for it. The improvements have been infinitesimal compared with what would have been achieved if a fraction of that had been spent on prevention in all its forms.

We already know or suspect what causes 80 to 90 per cent of cancers. The causes relate to diet, smoking, stress, and environmental factors. Yet we go on spending endless millions trying to find a magic cure when we could save many lives by spending a good slice of it on prevention and by changing food, economic and environmental policies so these causes of cancer are removed as much as possible.

We spend a fortune on heart transplants and cure technology which help relatively few, while more people than ever before are dying of heart disease for reasons that are preventable. Yet only five per cent of the Health Service budget goes on health education and the advertising budget of a multi-national food giant like Nestlé is bigger than that of the World Health Organisation.

Of course, there have been improvements in the treatment of some diseases and we applaud the researchers responsible, but these have been offset by the increases in cancer, heart disease, strokes, arthritis, other disabling problems, and those caused by stress and pollution. We could live much longer than we do and in much better health if we switched far more effort to prevention. Today, the rise in life expectancy has levelled out and for some is actually falling.

People will point to those living into their seventies, eighties and nineties, but more people are dying in middle age and many of those who live into later life suffer from disabling diseases. The story is the same in most parts of the developed world. Many might be living longer than they did 50 years ago but the population overall is becoming sicker. Our 'health' policies have become obsessed with the quantity of life and not the quality.

Dr. Vernon Coleman in his book, *The Health Scandal*, estimates that by 2020 the number of disabled and dependent people in the developed world will exceed the able bodied. He goes on: 'If you feel sceptical and suspect that this is alarmist, then let me just remind you that today, on average, one third of the population of any developed country has poor health which affects their ability to work or to look after themselves.'

We cannot go on as we are because the consequences will be horrific. We must change our values and principles in health care so those who live into old age are not disabled and dependent, but able to live life to the full as fit and healthy human beings. It can be done in the long term but not under the present system. Not a chance.

Profits from ill-health

The health services of the world are not always run for the benefit of patients, but for the multi-national drug companies. If you make your billions by selling drugs then the way to make even more money is to sell even more drugs. That means getting doctors to prescribe them and patients to insist on them. It's called economic growth. It is also exploitation on a mega scale.

The drug companies spend £200 million a year encouraging British doctors to prescribe their particular drugs. That works out on average at about £5,000 for every family doctor in the country. It can take the form of free gifts, free lunches, free trips abroad to 'conferences'. Against this bombardment of goodies, the NHS spends around £70 a *year* for each doctor to inform them about new drugs and their side-effects.

Most of the 'education' about new drugs the companies constantly unveil is given to the doctors by . . . the drug companies. Doctors get most of their medical education after they've qualified from events paid for by . . . the drug companies. Even the British Medical Association and members of the General Medical Council receive large sums of money from . . . the drug companies. The message is not so much 'Carry on doctor' as 'Carry on prescribing, doctor' – because that's good for profits if not for patients.

C. B. Zealley, the chairman of the Social Audit, had it right:

> We are not sensible about drugs. We use too many drugs and expect too much from them. We have been dazzled by the relatively few really effective products that have emerged mostly in the last 50 years. But instead of accepting these gratefully and recognising their limitations, we use drugs as if they could provide an answer to all our ills . . . It has led us, our doctors, the drug manufacturers and our governments into a mess of which no one can be proud.

The overuse of antibiotics, and particularly the blunderbuss variety aimed at a wide range of bugs, is also causing serious problems. Some bugs survive the treatment and as they breed pass on this resistance to their offspring. This is creating 'superbugs', and ever more powerful drugs with ever more unpleasant side-effects are needed to kill them. This is good for drug companies, but terrible for people. A chiropodist friend of mine knows of antibiotics being prescribed for the common corn!

The risk of treatment

A large, and increasing, number of hospital admissions has been estimated to be totally or partly due to adverse reaction to treatment. One study of antibiotics showed that 66 per cent of the time they were of doubtful value and when you added to that the adverse reactions that antibiotics can cause, the risks were greater than the chances of relief for many people. You then have more drugs being prescribed to counter the side effects of the first lot. This doesn't mean that no antibiotics should be prescribed, but it does mean that far fewer should be. What are we coming to when one of the fastest growing dangers to health is the very treatment that is supposed to make us well? And look what it is costing us. The NHS drugs bill is £1,500 million a year for nearly 400 million prescriptions.

The truth is that the large majority of illnesses (some say 80 per cent) require no drugs and no medical treatment. Our bodies can heal themselves if only they are given the chance. Swallowing pills can block the self-healing processes. What we need to do is to allow the chemical balance of our bodies to get back to how evolution planned it and then much of our disease can be overcome without medical intervention. That means fewer drugs, not more, and prescriptions when really necessary, not as a matter of course.

It means changing the way we live, what goes into our food, into our water, into our air, and reducing the kind of frustrations and anxieties that dominate life in our economic system. This is the only way to health. Drugs have a much smaller part to play.

The body's natural healing and preventative processes – like the immune system – can't work properly if the body is bombarded with drugs and the hundreds of thousands of human-made chemicals.

The whole body is thrown out of balance and doesn't work effectively. Hence more illness and, under the present system, more prescriptions.

The big killer

What do you think is the biggest killer in the rich world today? Cancer? Heart disease? Strokes? No. Stress. It is stress that fills the hospital beds, the waiting rooms, and the cemeteries. Stress-related disease is an epidemic that is threatening to overwhelm us. Those who are 'successful' die from stress-induced heart attacks, strokes and cancers, because of the pressure to compete with others who want to be even more 'successful'. Those who are the debris of the system, the unemployed and those in mind-numbing work, die from stress-induced heart attacks, strokes and cancers, because of the frustrations of life at the bottom of the pile. Lose hope and you can lose life.

The power of the human mind over the human body is immense and it can be used for good and bad. So the Green Party's policies involve treating the whole person, mind and body. If someone has an illness brought on by the stress of bringing up a family on a tiny income in a damp-ridden flat, then it is not a prescription for valium they want, but an adequate income and a better home. You can't divorce housing, pollution and economic policies from health. We are asking our doctors to prescribe away the deficiencies of the entire system, and they can't.

Many studies have shown how the power of the mind can affect the physical body. One report revealed that those recently widowed can be twelve times more likely to die than similar people who have not been bereaved. Stress and poor life-style brought on by unemployment also causes an enormous amount of illness and even kills. Figures have shown that when unemployment rises by a million, it coincides with a significant increase in the number of deaths and admissions to psychiatric hospitals. It is ridiculous to claim, as governments do, that unemployment and tedious, mindless, machine-minding work do not have a major impact on physical health. It's obvious they do, and it is governments who have the power to do something about that, not doctors. The body is not merely a mechanical machine. It is far more complex: until we accept this we will go on prescribing vast quantities of unnecessary drugs.

One other point about stress. We may live in the modern world, but our inner selves are virtually unchanged from the days when we used to hunt wild animals in the forests and grasslands. Evolution takes a long time and the 200 years of the industrial revolution is, to evolution, of no significance at all.

When we are frightened, frustrated, nervous or stressed in any way, our muscles tighten (which causes things like backaches and headaches), our hearts pump, and adrenalin flows. Back in the forests all those years ago, this was brought on by physical danger and would be released by physical action. We'd fight or run. The sort of circumstances that prompt these responses today are not released by physical action. You can't go round thumping the boss, whacking the machine with a hammer, or duffing up the gas man because you can't pay the bill. So this stress builds up within us, too often with deadly consequences. It is the unacceptable price we have to pay for having natural human characteristics in our unnatural, inhuman, system.

Some play sport to try to release this stress and tension, which is sensible, but the problem is more complex than that. We also have to remove other major sources of stress, like poverty, feelings of helplessness, and lack of control over events that affect our lives.

Removing the causes of illness

The answer as always is to change the system. I keep highlighting the connections between cause and effect, and this is another major example. If you have a new economic approach with new values and principles, you will reduce enormously the amount of illness we have to suffer. Green Party policies aim at reducing fear and insecurity (basic income), mindless work (human scale business and technology), unemployment (basic income, job sharing, more individual and creative production), and the need to 'succeed' by killing yourself (less emphasis on competition and more on co-operation). The quality of life would soar as people were given more power to control their own destiny.

If you add the policies I have already described on reducing pollution, ridding food of suspect additives and residues, cleaning up water supplies, and other preventative measures, you will appreciate what an impact we will have on health before a single prescription is dispensed and there will need to be considerably fewer of those.

A Green health policy would obviously need more resources spent on the NHS in the early years. There will be a time-lag between introducing prevention policies and seeing the results in fewer patients. In the meantime we still have to care for those made ill by the present attitudes to health. But in the longer term the money needed at the cure end of medicine would fall.

We would end the advertising of drugs to the public and the medical profession. Information on new drugs would be channelled through the medical schools and there would have to be independent scrutiny before drugs were allowed to be sold or prescribed. The listed drugs would be constantly monitored for usefulness and side effects.

We would move the emphasis from big centralised regional hospitals to care in the community wherever possible, either at smaller district hospitals, community hospitals, or in the home. People feel happier and are therefore more likely to recover in their own surroundings or in their own community than in some big, less personal hospital miles away. There would still be some specialisation in regional hospitals, but they would be the last resort of hospital care, not the first.

We must restructure the health service so it works much more closely with local and national government departments that deal with housing and social problems. They should be working together to identify the causes of illness and doctors should be able to make strong and effective recommendations to the authorities over the conditions that people have to live in. The doctors' role should change so they can get to the cause and their findings be acted upon. They should not simply be left to dispense drugs as the answer to everything. This means that doctors must be given more time with patients so that the background to physical or emotional illness can be talked out, and there must be actions that doctors can take when they have isolated the cause. If they believe the condition is caused by loneliness, as a lot of illness is, then there must be community carers who can take over from the doctor and find ways of overcoming that loneliness. This is the direction in which the Green Party would take our health service.

Health education would be taught throughout school life. Health centres would be expanded to play a major role in sickness prevention. We would expand those screening programmes that proved to be worthwhile (some are certainly not, despite what we are told), but we would put most of our efforts into showing people how to take care of their own health. Women who examine themselves for breast lumps, for instance, detect much more cancer at a curable stage than does an annual check-up at the clinic. If we are going to stop the onslaught of disease, people have to take responsibility for their own health care in terms of how they live and what they consume, but it is the government's responsibility to give them the information they need and the access to healthy food, water and air.

The Green Party would end the advertising of tobacco and alcohol. The dangers of smoking are well documented. The most effective single thing you can do to safeguard your health is not to smoke. But twenty per cent of all male admissions to general medical wards are alcohol-related. The government spends £344 trying to reduce alcohol consumption for every person who dies because of alcohol. For every person who dies from the abuse of illegal drugs, the government spends on anti-drug measures . . . £1,700,000. That is not to say that money should not be spent to stop the human tragedy of drug addiction, but it does mean the budget for reducing alcohol consumption is pathetic. The fact that the government gets more than £5 billion a year in tax from alcohol clearly impairs their judgement.

Here we hit on the main reason why prevention is not seen as better than cure; brass, loot, money. Stopping people getting ill is not good for business in the drug, tobacco, alcohol, food processing, meat and dairy industries, and many others. They all have tremendous influence in the corridors of power and they use it to head off any resistance to what they produce. Nor is prevention the glamorous end of medicine. But the truth is that while high technology can save the lives of a relative few, prevention on the scale the Green Party is talking about can prevent the premature deaths of many hundreds of thousands. That does not mean that all research into new cures would stop, but there would have to be a more sensible balance.

We would also have independent studies of alternative medicine. Those techniques which proved more, or as, effective as NHS treatments would be welcomed into the mainstream and be able to operate from health centres. There are charlatans in these areas (as there are in so-called orthodox medicine) and we would aim to weed them out and stop their exploitation. That said, I know from experience that some alternative techniques have a lot to offer and are certainly worthy of urgent and open minded research. One in particular I have come across, an advanced form of clinical ecology, has incredible potential.

Animal experiments

More than 144 million animal experiments have taken place in Britain alone since 1950 and every hour of every day another 20,000 creatures die in laboratories around the world. They die horribly in drug tests, they are shot through the head to test the effectiveness of weapons, they are poisoned, they are so mutilated that their bodies give up; and so it goes on. Some of the monkeys shot by high velocity bullets at Britain's Chemical Defence Laboratories at Porton Down took nearly three hours to die. Porton Down also tests nerve gas, hydrogen cyanide and such like on animals. Between 1952 and 1970, their Microbiological Research Centre used more than a thousand monkeys, almost 200,000 guinea pigs, and 1,250,000 mice.

There is the infamous LD50 test (the lethal dose of a substance needed to kill at least 50 per cent of the animals in the trial) which has been in wide use to test the goods we use in the kitchen, on the farm, in our gardens, on our faces and in industry. On average 60 animals are used each time and they are either injected, forced to breathe vapours, or have a tube inserted down the throat and the substance poured in.

Then there is the pain and anguish of 'life'. They have their eyes sewn up so they can't see, their limbs cut off, their eyes dosed with poisons. They are burned, starved and given severe electric shocks. One animal died of a blocked intestine after being force-fed the human equivalent of four pounds of lipstick formulation.

We are told that these abominations are justified because they have saved millions of human lives and further animal experiments will find new cures in the future. 'You can go on about animals', the predictable line goes, 'But what about the children these experiments help? Aren't people more important?'

As George Bernard Shaw once said: 'He who does not hesitate to vivisect will not hesitate to lie about it.'

Let me tell you the truth about these endless horrors inflicted on our fellow creatures. These experiments are next to useless. These animals are dying and suffering this incomprehensible agony for nothing. Not for children. Not for adults. For nothing. The fact is that the metabolism of animals is different from human beings and so they react differently. As Dr. Robert Sharpe pointed out in his exposé of vivisection, *The Cruel Deception*:

> . . . morphine sedates man, but stimulates cats; aspirin causes birth defects in rats and mice, but not in people; thalidomide

works the other way round; penicillin is highly toxic to guinea pigs and hamsters; the common industrial chemical benzine causes leukaemia in man but not in mice; insulin produces deformities in laboratory animals, but not in people; nitrophenol causes cataracts in humans, ducks and chicks, but not other laboratory animals; serotonin, a naturally occurring chemical in the body, raises the blood pressure in dogs, but reduces it in cats; and doses of aspirin used in human therapeutics actually poison cats whilst having no effect on the treatment of fever in horses.

Not only are animals as a whole different from humans in the way their bodies react, but they differ between species as well. All this makes animal experiments about as useful in medical 'research' as tossing a coin. Thalidomide, a drug to treat morning sickness, caused deformity in 10,000 babies after showing no ill-effects in any animal tests.

The arthritis drug, Opren, was tested on laboratory rats. It proved effective and had no side-effects. When it was given to humans there were 3,500 reports of adverse effects, many very serious, and 61 people died. And when ICI marketed Eraldin to treat heart conditions it sailed through the animal tests; in humans it turned out to cause eye damage, including blindness, and 23 people died.

These are just three cases from a very long list. If animal experiments can identify dangers to humans, how come that in just one year 120,366 of us either died from, or were admitted to hospital for, the side-effects of medicines? How come that up to 40 per cent of people prescribed drugs by their GP will suffer some adverse effects? And if the reaction is nausea, aches and pains, or psychological problems, how can an animal test reveal it? Only people can tell people about these things.

The way to test drugs or products for their potential harm to human beings is to test them on human tissue. Any other way is quite clearly a waste of time, highly dangerous, and when you look at how animals suffer, an affront to our humanity.

Yet we are told that without animal experiments we would not have rid this country of major killers like smallpox, cholera, typhoid and so on. Without vivisection we would not have developed the vaccines and drugs to combat them. Wrong again on two counts. First, as I've shown, animal tests are of no value because they are so unpredictable. It was not animals who produced the breakthroughs in these areas, but good judgement, good luck, and the study of human beings. Second, the effect of many vaccines and drugs has been negligible on the death rates which were all in rapid decline, and in many cases had been so for some time before medicine intervened. Indeed, if you look at the figures you see that the death rates often levelled off after the vaccines and drugs were introduced. Routine use of vaccine was ended in Sweden and West Germany without any increase in death or serious disease, which rather emphasises the point. Norway allows only 1,900 drug formulations while in Britain we have 18,000. Life expectancy in Norway is higher than in Britain. The World Health Organisation reckons that of the 60,000 drugs available on the world market, only 220 are really needed.

I am not saying that no vaccine or no drug is of any use, of course not. Some have been wonderful. I am saying, however, that the value of most of them has been overstated to a ridiculous degree and that animal experiments played no serious part in their development anyway. The evidence is overwhelming. Eighty-five per cent of the animal experiments carried out in the last 100 years have been done since 1950, yet 92 per cent of the decline in death rates happened *before* 1950! The vast majority of drugs we are given have come on to the market since 1950 as well. They have had a fantastic impact on drug company profits, but far less on the health of people.

Human tissue cultures, new computer models, and closely controlled clinical trials are the only ways to safely test drugs so they cannot harm large numbers of patients and to ensure that drugs that are bad for animals, but are useful to people, are not wrongly discarded. And if you want to reduce death rates and improve health, better living conditions are the most effective way.

The power of the drug barons

So why don't we do it instead of dispensing endless drugs and torturing animals? There are many reasons, none of them sound or decent, but all of them very powerful for the system. First the drug companies make enormous profits with margins of 30 per cent or often more. The chemical substance frusemide costs £5 for a thousand tablets, but was marketed by Hoechst under the brand name Lasix for £60 a thousand. The drug benzodiazepine costs £20 a kilo to make. The Swiss company Roche sell it to their sister company to market in the UK as valium. Cost: £922 a kilo. As we increase our intake of drugs, they increase their intake of money. Most of the drugs on the market and the new ones being introduced all the time add nothing to the health of the world. They are the 'me too' copycat drugs. One company markets a drug which sells well and as soon as the patent period runs out it's a free-for-all to produce a similar drug with a new brand name. You get stories in the papers about the wonderful properties of the new drug, the doctors will be bombarded with drug salesmen and glossy literature, and a fortune will be spent on the launch. Yet the drug will be nothing more than a direct 'steal' from a perfectly adequate drug already in use.

These irrelevant 'me-too's' also cost the lives of millions of animals every year – and will go on doing so until we have a government with the guts to take on the self-interest groups. The drug companies have always campaigned for vivisection because if you first persuade people that it is necessary (which they did), then the more animal tests you do the more responsible and safe you appear to be. It also looks better in a court of law when a drug kills or harms people. It is the same for food processing companies, cosmetics companies, the agro-chemical industry and others.

The researchers and scientists are to blame, too. Many animal experiments and the 'papers' that follow are done purely to further a career, not the quest for medical advancement. Some spend their whole lives experimenting on animals without going near a human patient. They earn their money testing for private companies and turning out useless 'research papers' which animals pay for with suffering and their lives. One paper revealed that if you starve animals they become more interested in food than sex. Brilliant eh? Then there was the Cambridge psychologist who blinded a monkey and spent six years studying her behaviour. Animal tests may not tell you much about human medicine, but they tell you an awful lot about some of the people who do them.

Then there is the government. Both Labour and Conservative administrations had the power to stop this slaughter, but they lacked the nerve or the inclination to do so. They support the drug industry because it adds to our balance of payments; it is a good export earner. As the government said about animal experimentation legislation in 1983:

> The United Kingdom has a large pharmaceutical industry which makes a large contribution to our balance of payments and employs 67,500 people. In devising new controls it is very important not to put industry at risk unnecessarily.

And when they were urged to ban the LD50 test, there was further confirmation of why animal experiments are supported in Westminster and Whitehall:

> LD50 results are required by drug regulating authorities in countries to which we export, contributing to a net favourable balance of trade in pharmaceuticals of over £500 million.

The Green Party would have the courage and conviction to

tackle these powerful groups. Animal experiments would be ended and the number of drugs would be reduced to what is necessary for people, not profit. Prevention would be our aim, not merely repair. Caring is also at the heart of the Green approach; instead of blowing our money on needless, over-priced drugs we would ensure that those with chronic illness or disability had the support and resources to realise their full potential. The way we treat our old and handicapped people in this country is outrageous.

A policy for health

We have to take a new direction in our thinking on health before the diseases of too much and too little destroy us. Fairness and foresight hold the key, not pharmaceuticals.

It's a remarkable fact that when doctors went on strike for a month in Israel the death rate dropped by fifty per cent – the biggest drop since the previous doctors' strike; doctors in Colombia refused to work for 52 days and the death rate fell by 30 per cent; a doctors' strike in Los Angeles coincided with an 18 per cent fall in the number of deaths. That is not to say that doctors have nothing to offer, quite the opposite, but that the system is so often forcing them to offer the wrong things. We need a new kind of doctor who has the time and the training to find the causes of ill health, and then has the ability to alert other agencies who can do something about it. Action, not re-action, will be our motto.

Then a Green Party health minister could stand up in the House of Commons and proclaim: 'We are treating fewer people than ever before because there are fewer people that need to be treated.'

Now that would *really* be a health policy.

13: Policy pointers

If your only tool is a hammer, all problems look like nails.
MARK TWAIN

I have not been able to cover all aspects of the Green approach in what is intended purely as an introduction. It will be useful, however, if I outline our thinking briefly in three other key areas before I finish.

HUMAN RIGHTS AND CIVIL LIBERTIES

Our personal freedoms are being constantly eroded. It is being done in piecemeal fashion, little by little, and many people don't realise it until they are victims themselves.

Britain, as the mother of parliaments, has always had a fine reputation around the world for defending the rights and freedoms of her citizens. That reputation is increasingly misplaced as the rights to silence, to join a trade union, of peaceful assembly, and to freedom of movement and expression, are gradually chipped away. Local government is forced to give up more and more of its powers to the few at the centre.

Clive Ponting, the former Ministry of Defence civil servant, was prosecuted for telling the public that the government were lieing to them. Only a sensible jury kept him out of prison. Since then he has uncovered many examples of the sinister way this country is being run.

There was the story of the woman who lost a job because the police, MI5 and the Special Branch told her prospective employer, a defence contractor, that her car had been seen near a 'subversive meeting'. She had not been at the meeting, she had just parked her car unknowingly in that area. Officers in plain clothes had then come along taking down all the car numbers near the arts centre where the meeting was held. They traced the owners' names through the vehicle licensing centre at Swansea and made notes on their security files. The woman lost the job for parking her car in the wrong place at the wrong time, and as the area is popular for restaurants and a cinema, she would not have been the only innocent party.

And what was this 'subversive meeting' that warranted all this attention from our police and security forces? A public meeting of the Freedom of Information Campaign addressed by MPs, members of the House of Lords, and newspaper editors!

Ponting also tells the tale of a couple who came back to find their home ransacked. Papers were everywhere, but nothing was stolen – even though there were some valuable items they could have taken. The police found good fingerprints and said they were confident of an early arrest. Then they went quiet and closed the file. It turned out that MI5 and the Special Branch had made a blunder. They had been given a warrant by the Home Secretary to search the house of someone of the same name a few streets away. They had confused the addresses. The man they wanted was a 'subversive' because he was a member of several environmental groups and was leading a campaign against a nuclear power station. They wanted to break into his house to find out who was funding the campaign.

These are not isolated examples. Phone taps have become a matter of course and there is no way you can find out if it is happening to you. Big Brother isn't some distant danger. He is here.

If anyone needs final confirmation of that they should look at the new Official Secrets Act which prevents the passing of official information to the public under any circumstances without government permission. The defence that such action is in the national interest, which saved Clive Ponting, is no longer allowed. Most official secrets law is not there to keep information from other countries. They know most of it anyway. It is there and is being tightened to keep the truth from us, the people of the UK.

It means that even if the government is lying through its teeth, it is an offence to supply the official information to prove it. As Ponting says, the new law 'enables any government to cover up incompetence, deceit, or even corruption and illegality.'

The Green Party would introduce a Freedom of Information Act to give the public access to all information except that truly needed for national security, which is a fraction of that covered by present legislation. There would be a Bill of Rights and Civil Liberties to cover all our freedoms and ensure that governments could not behave in a way that eroded them. We must not allow complacency to take away the freedoms our ancestors fought so hard to secure. Public complacency and authoritarian governments are a dangerous combination.

I am reminded of what Pastor Niemoeller, a victim of the Nazis, once said:

First they came for the communists and I did not speak out
because I was not a communist.
     Then they came for the trade unionists and I did not speak
out because I was not a trade unionist.
     Then they came for me and there was no one left to speak
out for me.

We must speak out and defend all our freedoms for ourselves and others. If we don't, one day we will open our eyes and see how many we have lost.

EDUCATION

The conventional view of education is far too narrow. It concentrates on our early years and then lets us get on with it. What we should be doing is giving access to education to everyone throughout their lives as and when they want it. You don't stop learning when you enter your twenties and it is often long after the teenage years that people appreciate the benefits of education and develop a thirst for learning.

Basic Income would be increased for those who wanted to take time away from a job at any time in their life to learn new skills and gain new knowledge. Opportunities to do that would be made widely available.

Conventional education is too narrow in another sense, too. It leads increasingly to more and more specialisation and this limits a person's ability to be independent and self-reliant. I've said before that some skills and knowledge are useless to us away from the workplace. Schools should be developing fully rounded young people who have a range of practical skills to complement their mental abilities. Too much specialisation can also cloud judgement and vision by concentrating the mind on one small area of life at the expense of seeing the whole picture. I am not saying that specialising in one sphere of interest is wrong as such – but a thorough base must be built first.

Green education would aim for smaller schools and classes so learning was on a close, personal level. Village schools would not close and many would re-open. Big urban schools would be encouraged to break up into smaller units. We want an education system that does not force teachers through weight of numbers to stand in front of big classes just talking at the children and students. The units must be small enough to ensure a sense of belonging and to allow everyone's natural talents and creativity to play a part in the classroom. We must bring education alive by involving students at all times in the learning process.

The present system makes its educational decisions in the way it makes all its decisions – within a severely limited definition of what is most 'economic'. In short: how much does it cost? What it doesn't see is that if you give young people a sense of belonging, personal worth, and respect for the community you can massively reduce violence and vandalism. Doesn't that make this approach more 'economic' overall even if it means spending more money on schools and teachers to achieve it?

Green schools would also be used to help re-build the sense of community that industrialism has done so much to erode. We would encourage all sections of the community to play a part in school life. Older people have a lifetime of experience and knowledge they could share with children and students. We would have education centres with a wide age range. The more interaction we can achieve between generations the better. I remember meeting one man in his seventies who had changed his entire attitude towards young people since he went to college as a mature student. Woe betide anyone who criticised the young when he was around!

Power over the schools' finances and curriculum would be handed to individual schools and governing bodies made up of teachers, other school employees, parents, the students themselves and representatives of the community. Once again, this would give power to people to make their own decisions. We reject the idea that you can solve every problem and meet every need with one all-encompassing answer dictated from above. A Green society, and particularly education, will be flexible and to achieve that you need local decision-making that can react to individual circumstances.

Today education is not flexible. It moulds people for the system when we should be moulding the system to the needs and talents of people. Green education policy would develop and encourage all these abilities. We would celebrate the spectacular diversity of human potential, not turn out units of production.

HOUSING

One of the most offensive sights in Britain is people sleeping in cardboard boxes on a freezing winter's night while all over the city are unoccupied buildings. No civilised government would let this happen.

There are many hundreds of thousands of empty houses in Britain and these would be made available to give shelter to the homeless. It is absurd that we are covering so much green land with concrete while these houses go unused or inner city land lies untouched as speculators wait for the price to go up. We would make holding on to empty houses and unused inner-city building land unprofitable through the Community Ground Rent. CGR would also slow down land prices as the speculator became part of history.

Our housing policy is aimed first at the renovation and repair of existing buildings. New ones would only be built where necessary for need, not greed. Planning permission would only be given for new housing where the local need for it could be proved and it would be built for the homeless – not for those who have the money to live where they like. Look at all the land lost to new housing in the last decade – yet there are more homeless people than ever. Why? Because the homes have been built for the highest profit, not for people who need them.

We would take action to discourage second homes. How can it be right that people have holiday homes on the Isle of Wight and elsewhere while local people can't find a place to live? The houses that were built would have to meet far higher standards than we have today. Buildings would be designed to use as little energy as possible and to last as long as possible. We have pulled down millions of buildings in mis-guided redevelopment schemes and within less than 20 years the new homes have been as bad as the slums we spent a fortune replacing. If we build for quality that will not happen and if you take the longer view it would turn out cheaper, as well as using less energy and fewer resources than the build-and-bulldoze policies of the last 40 years.

There would be grants and expert support for individuals and communities to build homes for themselves; we would aim at a mix of housing, for sale and rent, public and private, that gave everyone shelter. Greens believe that a decent home is a basic human right and there will be housing additions to Basic Income for those who need it to make sure no one must sleep rough. Cardboard boxes have no place in a Green housing policy.

I have described here the broad outline of our approach if the population continues to rise. If we are successful in persuading people it is better to have fewer children, then, of course, the pressure for housing will diminish much quicker.

The built environment

Housing and buildings are not just places to live and work in. For most people they make up most of the scenery. Therefore what they look like is of fundamental importance. Most, and I mean most, of the building designs of the past fifty years have been ghastly. The high-rise concrete and low-budget techniques have produced areas of our urban landscape that are offensive to the eye. This is even more incomprehensible when you think of some of the lovely buildings they replaced in a process that still goes on today as quality is demolished for the bland, the boring, and the make-as-much-profit-as-you-can. In an ever changing world, to have buildings that we grew up with or which have been there for a long time is very important to us, though we might not always appreciate that until the bulldozers arrive. I have seen people in tears when their old schools have been knocked down even though they left them 40 and 50 years before. They cried because so many memories were being demolished with the bricks and mortar. Part of them was disappearing, too.

Greens appreciate the emotional attachment that can develop between people and familiar buildings, the sense of stability they give us. Our policies reflect that understanding.

Our commitment to repair the old before building the new will slow down dramatically the redevelopment mania that has been so destructive and to a large degree unnecessary. Listed buildings will be protected much more vigorously than they are today.

Local councils and governments, sometimes with the best of intentions, have been responsible for what can only be described as municipal vandalism in our villages, towns and cities.

It is time to say enough.

14: Summon the spirit

Progress should not speed man faster than his soul.
CHINESE PROVERB

There is yet another fundamental dimension to the Green vision which is unique to politics. It recognises that human beings are not consumption machines. We have a soul.

It is our soul, our life-force, our spirit deep within us, call it what you like, that has been suppressed, often extinguished, by the demands of the system which denies the existence of anything that can't be seen, touched, measured or turned into money.

It is our soul that is moved by beauty, nature, art, words, and emotion. Why do so many detest massive, modern concrete buildings? Why do we love buildings of charm and character? Because we have a soul. Without it, we could not care less what they looked like. There is so much more to human beings, so much potential that remains untapped just because our system ridicules any suggestion that such potential exists. If Blackie the heifer could find her calf unaided all those miles away simply through instinct, then just think of the true potential of the human instinct, the human mind, if only we would recognise the possibility.

A crisis of the soul

Our souls have been imprisoned since the start of the industrial revolution. Since then only a tiny fraction of our potential has been used, the bit we need to make and demand material 'things'. Our emotional and spiritual needs have been ignored because grey politics and economics cannot be expected to address what they refuse to believe even exist. Our souls have become trapped and tortured inside us, resulting in depression, despair, a lack of fulfilment, and a deep sense that 'there must be more to life than this'.

It is not only an environmental crisis we face, but a crisis of the soul, and they cannot be separated. The cause of both is the same.

Suicide is the third most common cause of death in adults under 35 and suicide among teenagers is increasing alarmingly. It is ten times more common for children to try to take their own life than a generation ago. Well over 100,000 people attempt suicide in Britain every year. Alcoholism and drug addiction go on increasing, as do violent crime and other social disorders. Much of our 'growth' is the money spent reacting to the emotional warfare going on inside millions of people. It will go on getting worse as the system blunders forth to new depths of inhumanity.

It doesn't have to be like this.

As the Bible says: 'What shall it profit a man if he shall gain the whole world and lose his own soul?'

I have met people who have used the system to the full, the lucky few with all the 'things', and even they are slowly seeing the emptiness of it all. I am not surprised. They have had the wealth to take the system to its conclusion, to chase the material dream, and after buying everything they have ever desired, they realise that it was all an expensive illusion. You can't buy happiness and you don't need to. Freeing the soul costs nothing but a change of values.

Just say to yourself:

I will not judge people by what they own, but by what they are.

I will not judge anyone by their race, colour, creed, or sexual orientation.

I will not take any notice of people who judge me by false values.

I do not see people with many material possessions and a big income as more successful than those who have less.

I will not judge my own success on that basis, either.

I do not believe that people should live in poverty while others get richer and richer and I will do all I can to end that injustice.

I will not knowingly harm or cause suffering to any human being or any of our fellow creatures with which we share the Earth.

I reject violence in all its forms, including emotional violence.

I believe it is our duty to help others in every way we can and to leave the natural world at least as diverse and healthy as when we found it.

These are just a few of the new values that will free us from the cycle of environmental and emotional degradation that threatens to overwhelm us. I promise you from my own experience that if you make that commitment and stick to it, you are rewarded with a new sense of happiness, contentment, and sense of mental stability and wellbeing.

The ancient warnings

We were warned long ago of the folly we had embarked upon and the warnings didn't come from scientists or government ministers. They came from the ancient cultures of the world which appreciate what is really important to life and emotional well-being – and it isn't cars, fridges and ghetto blasters, or having more than the next-door neighbour.

I remember when I was very young there was a cowboy film on the television every Sunday afternoon. It nearly always ended with the cavalry coming over the hill to save the day and sort out the Indians. The bugle sounded and I cheered because the 'good guys' had arrived. That is what I was supposed to think. Indians didn't make the movies, the system did. You learn, however, that the so-called backward peoples, the American Indians, the Aborigines, the people of the rainforests, and all those like them, know more than we will ever know about the Earth and the spiritual and emotional links we have with all creation. We are clever. They are wise.

I have already mentioned that stunning American Indian prophecy about the Warriors of the Rainbow. Here is another piece of Indian wisdom from which we must learn, and fast . . . In 1855, the United States government made an offer for an area of Indian land. Had they been part of our system the Indians would have tried to squeeze every cent out of the government that they possibly could. Instead, Chief Seattle of the Dwamish Indians told a shocked and, of course, bewildered government:

> How can you buy or sell the sky? We do not own the freshness of the air or the sparkle on the water. How then can you buy them from us? Every part of the Earth is sacred to my people, holy in their memory and experience. We know the white man does not understand our ways. He is a stranger who comes in the night, and takes from the land whatever he needs. The Earth is not his friend, but his enemy, and when he's conquered it, he moves on. He kidnaps the Earth from his children. His appetite will devour the earth and leave behind a desert. If the beasts were gone, we would die from a great loneliness of the spirit, for whatever befalls the Earth, befalls the children of the earth.

Not bad for a 'backward' Indian, is it? But did we learn from this great wisdom? Did we listen? No, we condemned them as savages, took their lands, destroyed their culture and their inherited wisdom, forced them to conform – and we are still doing it today all over the Earth from Australia to the Far East to Brazil to Africa and the United States.

The Green Party does not want to destroy the diversity of human cultures, but to celebrate them. We recognise that all cultures have something we can learn from because of the sheer volume of experiences that have developed them, sometimes over thousands of years. The traditional cultures recognise our links with nature and our emotional needs, but as our modern culture has become ever more dominant, so those links and needs have been ignored with the social and human consequences I've described. To put this right, the Earth must first become our friend again and not our enemy. From that, all else will flow.

We will encourage diversity of life-style, which will develop as we hand power to communities and regions and stop dictating everything from above. The Green Party will promote and support efforts to retain and recapture the traditional culture of countries and regions within the UK and, through our aid and foreign policies, further afield. It is not a case of going back, but of mixing the wisdom of the past with the knowledge of the present. If we are to do this, the tidal wave of what you might call Coca Colaism must be repelled.

Greens appreciate that, emotionally, people prefer smaller groups where there is personal contact. We get lost, lonely and uncomfortable when any organisation gets too large, distant, and impersonal. Very few people are lonely in a village compared with a city. In the cities there may be a lot more people, but there is less contact between them. People get lost in the rush and the numbers. It's all too big.

For most of the evolution of humankind, we lived in small groups, the tribes and the villages. The world around us has changed beyond belief since then, but our emotions, what goes on inside us, has hardly changed at all. Our physical bodies may walk around in our modern environment, but our inner selves, our natural responses and needs, were developed in very different circumstances and surroundings. The Stone Age meets Star Wars, if you like! No wonder emotional problems and the illness that stems from them are now an epidemic in developed countries. It also explains why there are many millions of small groups where people meet or play together, everything from the sports club, to the knitting circle, the horticultural society, and the local gang. We feel more comfortable and secure in these groups on a human scale and governments must appreciate that in all their policies.

Feminine values

The most important aspects of our emotions, however, in terms of environmental destruction and much else, are what Greens call *feminine values*. This can be misleading because both men and women have these values and emotions, but they come much easier and in greater abundance to most women, with the odd exception. Let's get it straight. Women are not destroying the world. Men are. It is men who control the world in almost every aspect of life and it is their values of aggression, competition, dominance and power that have brought about our environmental and emotional downfall. Men and male values are killing the Earth.

It is no accident that Margaret Thatcher became Britain's first woman Prime Minister by having more of these male values than her male colleagues. It was she who promoted the live-for-today, live-for-yourself, aggressive go-getter as the role model for all of us to emulate and admire. More and more for me, me, me, is the motivation of Thatcherism. That's tragic for so many reasons, not least because she has done women a terrible disservice,

The fact is we need more truly feminine values at the heart of all decision making. So many women are quick to appreciate what the Green Party is saying because the emotions of caring, sharing, and protecting are so natural to them and these are the emotions that must prevail if we are to leave our children a future. I stress again, they are not exclusive to women. Men have them, too, but they are not encouraged by the system to free their emotions and show them. From the time we are toddlers we males are told that big boys don't cry, we are given aggressive toys like guns and jet fighters, and told we must be strong and compete in all we do. Television confirms this stereotype every day, and the gentler side of our nature is suppressed. Much bad behaviour is blamed on human nature when the nature of humans is shaped by the very society that complains about it.

The Green Party would build a society that balanced these male-female values so that the positive sides of both were encouraged for the good of the community. There is no balance today. Machismo is out of control.

We are the only political party that campaigns for such things. The others talk about competing everywhere when what we should be doing is asking how we can reduce competition that is wasteful and unnecessary and replace it with co-operation, sharing, caring, and a sense of personal worth for all. We can do it if we really want to. What's the alternative? Even fiercer competition, more growth, more suicides, more emotional illness, more violence?

Schumacher could see the connection clearly.

> I suggest that the foundations of peace cannot be laid by universal prosperity, in the modern sense, because such prosperity, if attainable at all, is attainable only by cultivating such drives of human nature as greed and envy, which destroy intelligence, happiness, serenity and thereby . . . peacefulness . . .

Green politics. Politics as if people mattered. That's the only way to save our souls.

15: The whole world in our hands

A brighter dawn awaits the human day, When poverty and wealth, the thirst of fame, The fear of infamy, disease and woe, War with its million horrors and fierce hell, Shall live but in the memory of time.
PERCY BYSSHE SHELLEY

There is no greater force known to man than an idea whose time has come.
VICTOR HUGO

It is a sobering thought that we, the generations alive today, are probably the last generations that can secure the future of life on Earth.

By the time the last of us has gone, the battle will be won or lost. By then the changes will have been made that will heal the planet or the fundamental damage will be beyond repair and life will be an increasingly unpleasant and tenuous existence.

Quite something to contemplate, isn't it, that it's all down to us? But it should not frighten us, it should inspire us, for no other people in history have been given a challenge such as this.

Life itself depends on what we do these next 50 years, but the answers await us if only we will lift our eyes and our hearts and embrace them.

Some will undoubtedly take the ostrich approach, ignore all the warnings, and carry on as if nothing is wrong. Those who want to do that will go on supporting one of the grey political parties and playing the game by the rules of the grey economic system.

They will go on believing that you can expand forever in a

finite area and that fragile life support processes can survive any amount of punishment. They will go on believing that you achieve peace by preparing for war and that more 'things' mean more happiness.

But they must also look their children in the eyes and justify what they do, because it is the children who must live with the consequences of what we do, or don't do, today. We must understand that if the obsession with more and more destroys the Earth's capacity to provide, then more and more will lead to less and less for everyone, and eventually to nothing.

Some people will go on ignoring all this in the hope that it will go away, but I am enormously encouraged by what is beginning to happen and I think there is an excellent chance that sanity is breaking out just in time.

There is a quiet, peaceful revolution taking place in the hearts and minds of millions of people in this country and hundreds of millions more around this world we all share. It is the dawning of a new age of consciousness about our links with the rest of creation and how we are so physically and emotionally dependent upon them. Those millions are making their peace, their Green peace, with the planet and all the glorious expressions of life that nature has woven in all their magnificence.

They know that Green politics will not just mean a safer life, but a better, more satisfying one. They know it is our only chance. The suicide note does not have to be signed, the dragon can be tamed, it doesn't have to be like this, but we must start *today*.

It has taken me about three months to write this book and in the time between first word and last an area of irreplaceable tropical forest 90 times the size of the Isle of Wight has been destroyed or degraded. A similar area has returned to desert. Eighteen billion tonnes of topsoil have been lost through erosion. At least ninety species have become extinct, probably many more. And nine million people, nearly half of them children, have died from hunger-related disease.

When they see figures like that, surely people can no longer argue with what the Green Party has been saying since the moment it was formed: that the human race is in serious trouble because the needs of people and of the planet and the needs of the system are in permanent and potentially fatal contradiction.

I want to end with the words, not of a politician, but those of a highly respected member of my profession, David Attenborough, spoken at the end of his series, 'The Living Planet'. He said that on the evidence before us, human beings could clearly devastate the Earth. If we were not to do so, he said, we must have a plan. These are David's words, and they represent the very minimum we have to do:

> One. We should not so exploit natural resources that we destroy them . . . common sense you might think and yet look what we've done to the European herring and are still doing to other species.
>
> Two. We should not interfere with the basic processes of life on which all life depends, in the sky, on the green surface of the Earth and in the sea . . . and yet we go on pouring our poisons into the sky, cutting down tropical rainforests, dumping our rubbish into the oceans.
>
> And third. We should preserve the diversity of life not just because we depend upon it for our food, though we do, nor because we know so little about it that we don't know what we're losing, though that's the case as well. But it is surely that we have no moral right to destroy other living organisms with which we share the Earth.
>
> As far as we know, the Earth is the only place in the universe where there is life. Its continued survival now rests in our hands.

All I can add is that in the next fifty years, unless we change, we will eliminate a third of life on Earth and species will become extinct, not even at the rate of one a day, but one a *minute*.

Never has it been more clear that we don't inherit the Earth from our ancestors, we borrow it from our children. Never has it been more urgent to accept that we must live more simply so others may simply live.

Children don't have a vote, grandchildren don't have a vote, starving children don't have a vote, wildlife and rainforests don't have a vote. But we have a vote and we can use it to vote for them. Join us, support us, the only political movement that doesn't literally cost the Earth.

The present economic system and the grey political parties that support and promote it are at war with the planet, at war with our children and at war with the future.

The Green Party would like to make peace.

Further reading

I am grateful for numerous reports and articles which have applied the facts and figures in each chapter and for the following books which I strongly recommend if you would like to take the various issues on from here.

Economics

The Living Economy, edited by Paul Ekins, Routledge and Kegan Paul.
After the Crash, Guy Dauncey, Green Print.
The Race for Riches, Jeremy Seabrook, Green Print.
Small is Beautiful, E. F. Schumacher, Sphere Books.
Good Work, E. F. Schumacher, Sphere Books.

Aid, trade and Third World development

Developed to Death, Ted Trainer, Green Print.
Food, Need, Greed and Myopia, Geoffrey Yates, Earthright Publications.
A Fate Worse Than Debt, Susan George, Penguin Books.
Real Aid: Missed Opportunities, Report by the Independent Group on British Aid.
For Richer For Poorer, John Clark, Oxfam Publications.
Nicaragua: The Threat of a Good Example? Dianna Melrose, Oxfam Publications.
Modernising Hunger, Phillip Raikes, Heinemann.

Population

Population Today, Eric McGraw, Kaye and Ward.
Human Numbers And Human Needs, Paul Harrison and John Rowley, International Planned Parenthood Federation.
Annual Report. Population Concern.

Agriculture and farming

Red or Green for Farmers? Richard Body, Broad Leys Publishing.
Living Without Cruelty, Mark Gold, Green Print.
Far From Paradise, John Seymour and Herbert Girardet, Green Print.
Silent Spring, Rachel Carson, Penguin Books

Energy

Energy Without End, Michael Flood, Friends of the Earth.
The Greenhouse Effect, Stewart Boyle and John Ardill, New English
    Library.
No Immediate Danger, Rosalie Bertell, The Women's Press.
Atomic Crossroads, John Valentine, Merlin Press.
Acid Rain, Steve Elsworth, Pluto Press.

Transport

Wheels Within Wheels, Mick Hamer, Routledge and Kegan Paul.

Defence and the arms trade

Without the Bomb, Alternative Defence Commission, Paladin.
Towards the Final Abyss? Professor Michael Pentz, J.D. Bernal Peace
    Library.
Over Here: The US Military Presence in Britain, Paul Rogers, CND
    Publication.
Nato In or Out, Various, CND Publications.
Death on Delivery, Campaign Against the Arms Trade.
Bombs for Breakfast, Committee on Poverty and the Arms Trade.
Does Britain Contribute to Torture and Murder? Amnesty Inter-
    national.

Health and animal research

The Health Scandal, Dr. Vernon Coleman, Mandarin.
The Cruel Deception, Dr. Robert Sharpe, Thorsons.

General

The Earth Report, edited by Edward Goldsmith and Nicholas Hildyard,
    Mitchell Beazley.

Battle for The Planet, André Singer, Pan Books.

Green Britain or Industrial Wasteland? Edited by Edward Goldsmith and Nicholas Hildyard, Polity Press.

Seeing Green, Jonathon Porritt, Blackwell.

A Green Manifesto, Sandy Irvine and Alec Ponton, Optima.

The Stolen Future, Patrick Rivers, Green Print.

Fight for the Forest: Chico Mendes in his own words, Latin America Bureau.

In the Rainforest, Catherine Caufield, Picador.

Earthrights, Kogan Page/The World Wide Fund for Nature.

The Green Party

If, after reading this book, you would like to know more about the Green Party, its aims and policies, write to:

The Green Party
FREEPOST
London SW12 9YY

Green Print

Green Print is an independent publisher of books on green issues, or written from a radical green perspective. Our recent and best-selling titles include *Living Without Cruelty* by Mark Gold, which has become the standard presentation of the case for vegetarianism and animal rights; *C for Chemicals* by Mike Birkin and Brian Price, a handy guide to chemical hazards in the home and garden and how to avoid them; *After the Crash* by Guy Dauncey, which shows how green economics is taking effect at the grassroots around the world; *Teaching Green* by Damian Randle, which sets out the theory and – above all – the practice of green education for parents and teachers alike; and *Nitrates* by Nigel Dudley, explaining for lay readers the threat of agricultural fertilisers to our food and water supplies.

Our series of *Green Guides* now includes guides to England, Scotland and France.

To receive our catalogue, phone us on 071–267 3399, or write to Green Print (ID), 10 Malden Road, London NW5 3HR.